Claus Detjen

The Responsibility of a Founding Father

Claus Detjen

The Responsibility of a Founding Father

Reinhold Würth –
Dialogues with an Entrepreneur and Patron

𝔉𝔯𝔞𝔫𝔨𝔣𝔲𝔯𝔱𝔢𝔯 𝔄𝔩𝔩𝔤𝔢𝔪𝔢𝔦𝔫𝔢 **Buch**

Bibliographical information of the Deutsche Nationalbibliothek
(German National Library)
The German National Library catalogues this publication in the
German National Bibliography; detailed bibliographic information
can be found on the website: http://dnb.ddb.de.

Claus Detjen
The Responsibility of a Founding Father
Reinhold Würth – Dialogues with an Entrepreneur and Patron

Frankfurter Societäts-Medien GmbH
Frankenallee 71–81
60327 Frankfurt am Main, Germany
General Manager: Oliver Rohloff

First Edition
Frankfurt am Main 2015

ISBN 978-3-95601-107-8

Frankfurter Allgemeine Buch

Copyright	Frankfurter Societäts-Medien GmbH
	Frankenallee 71–81
	60327 Frankfurt Frankfurt Business Media GmbH –
	Der F.A.Z.-Fachverlag, 60327 Frankfurt am Main, Germany
Cover	Anja Desch, Frankfurt am Main, Germany
Cover photo	© Andi Schmid
Typesetting	Wolfgang Barus, Frankfurt am Main, Germany
Printed by	Kösel GmbH & Co. KG, Am Buchweg 1, 87452 Altusried-Krugzell, Germany
Translated by:	Geraldine Diserens
Original title:	Der Patriarch in seiner Verantwortung
	Reinhold Würth – Gespräche mit dem Unternehmer und Mäzen

All rights reserved.

Contents

Preface and Acknowledgements	7
The outside view. On R.W.'s 80th birthday Hans Magnus Enzensberger	9
Reinhold Würth: A tentative approach Claus Detjen	11
Chapter 1: The founding father makes provisions The family will retain the management	19
Chapter 2: In a world that has come off the rails The businessman has to know what is happening in politics	41
Chapter 3: Appeal for a United States of Europe Europe needs a fiscal equalisation scheme	57
Chapter 4: The free entrepreneur and politics In the liberalist tradition	75
Chapter 5: On the responsibility of the media Who supervises the watchdogs?	101
Chapter 6: Commercial traveller, pilot, mariner, hiker Philosophy of life: *Vibrant Curiosity*	111
Chapter 7: What the next generation should be spared Extreme existential experiences	135
Chapter 8: Reinhold Würth the Christian There is solace and hope in faith	147
Chapter 9: Dialogue with Bettina Würth Women manage differently	163
Publications by Reinhold Würth	173
Books about Reinhold Würth	184
Curriculum vitae Prof. Dr. h.c. Reinhold Würth	185
The author	189

Preface and Acknowledgements

This book is tied to a date and a person. Entrepreneur Reinhold Würth will turn eighty in April 2015. A festive occasion for a book that is dedicated to the entrepreneur, but which does not follow the festschrift model. In this book, Reinhold Würth speaks for himself; in dialogues with the author, he gives insights into the ideas and positions that determine the citizen, the patron and the family man in his understanding of responsibility above and beyond the role of the entrepreneur. German author and poet Hans Magnus Enzensberger makes Reinhold Würth's personality accessible to the reader with an incisive character sketch through the wing mirror.

There is no lack of publications about and by Reinhold Würth. However, up to this point, he has never spoken out so comprehensively and eclectically about his vision of a United States of Europe, his criticism of Germany's policy towards Russia, his roots in southern German liberalism, his aloofness from the media, his faith in the Creator and about the arrangements he has made for the Würth Group beyond his own lifetime. The businessman and art collector Reinhold Würth reveals himself in these dialogues as a political animal.

Reinhold Würth allocated a lot of his precious time to this book. The dialogues took place in the course of 2014 in his office in Künzelsau, supplemented by amendments in 2015, encounters at exhibition openings, at anniversary celebrations and on trips. In the text version of the book, the questions that the author asked are written in italics above Reinhold Würth's answers.

I greatly appreciate the patience, the openness, the humour and the unique form of clarity that I have experienced with Reinhold Würth. This enabled an eclectic dialogue to develop between two unconnected people who belong to the generation that was shaped by wartime and the post-war era.

I would like to thank Bettina Würth, Chairwoman of the Advisory Board of the Würth Group, for granting insights into her management principles as her father's successor during a separate interview.

The author received advice and support in generous measure from C. Sylvia Weber, Head of the Business Unit Art in the Würth Group; I owe her a particular debt of gratitude. Likewise Norbert Bamberger, Reinhold Würth's personal assistant, whose attention to detail during the final corrections was indispensable. As with all books, the attentiveness and competence of the responsible person at the publishing house, the Publishing Manager of Frankfurter Allgemeine Buch, Danja Hetjens, lies unseen behind this one too, and I would like to express my deepest gratitude to her.

Claus Detjen
March 2015

The outside view. On R.W.'s 80th birthday

Hans Magnus Enzensberger

It is not easy to say something about Reinhold Würth in a few sentences. Looking him up in *Who's Who* does not help either. It tells us more than enough about his successes, but not about how strong-willed and reserved he is, generous and vigilant, deeply rooted in his heritage, but expanding worldwide, approachable, but cautious at a distance. But: What outsider would be able to make sense of all of these things that he can guess at?

And it continues in this vein. We know that this *paterfamilias* knows his people and looks after them, irrespective of what rank they hold in his companies. But he only trusts a small few confidants. Because he is rich, everyone wants money from him. He gives away a lot of what he has, but he does not give a farthing for the sycophants. Money is not the most interesting aspect about him.

Although he has hardly missed one technical innovation, he does not think much of the zeitgeist. He watches fashions pass him by with certain irony. He prefers to adhere to old remnants. In this sense, he is a traditionalist.

Anyone who has observed him at events, meetings, conferences and other rituals notices that he often says nothing at all for a quarter of an hour. He knows the speeches that extol what he has achieved. Maybe such palaver bores him. But as soon as certain key words are uttered, as soon as objections or opportunities are indicated, he is instantly wide awake again.

I hardly dare to say it, but did he not more or less involuntarily take over an abandoned role in the administrative district of Hohenlohe? Among the many princes and counts in the region, there were not only oppressors of the peasantry, but also enlightened patriarchs, prominent collectors and ambitious developers. Würth is a self-made man. But even the noblemen of old started off small too. It was just a little further back in time. Our man can rival them, and not only in this little administrative district, but on more than one continent. He has built subsidiaries, museums and even a luxury hotel. These ambitious buildings can be viewed in a book. *Building for the World* is the name of the illustrated book. However, the desire to get involved as a developer is not solely rooted in feudalism. The old bourgeoisie shared this passion. The Free Imperial City of Schwäbisch Hall can also boast dynasties with whom Würth is on a par.

He values his independence. He never wanted to list on the stock exchange. He distrusts the practices of the financial sector just as much as he does managers who change their company as easily as their shirt. He thought long term right from the start. He wanted as much as possible of what he had achieved to outlive him. He ensured this would happen too.

I am always happy to meet him, but I know him too little. Many who know better, friends and competitors, employees and adversaries, could say far more about him than me. But there will always be a remainder that Reinhold Würth prefers to keep to himself.

Reinhold Würth: A tentative approach

Claus Detjen

Reinhold Würth is known throughout Europe as an entrepreneur, an art collector, and a patron. In Reinhold Würth's life achievements, the reader makes the acquaintance of an entrepreneur whose success can be regarded as prototypical for Germany's rise to become Europe's leading economic powerhouse. It was not state-owned enterprises or money-making machines run by financial conglomerates that brought about the German economic miracle after World War II, but entrepreneurs like Reinhold Würth and their employees.

He lives with and in the globally operating company which he created. He wants to retain the Würth Group in family ownership. It is among the 91 percent of all German companies which are family-controlled and which generate more than 50 percent of the total revenue of German business.

Reinhold Würth practices his philanthropic activities in the sense of a peculiarity of the German Basic Law (the German constitution): Ownership is a social obligation within society. He is a passionate advocate of the unification of Europe; he envisions a United States of Europe. German Foreign Minister Frank-Walter Steinmeier paid tribute to this dedication on the part of Reinhold Würth as meritorious on the latter's 80th birthday.

However, Reinhold Würth is not an active politician. "I am glad that I am not a politician," he concedes. He prefers the independence of the entrepreneur; it gives him the freedom to demand liberalism as a guiding principle for sensible politics. This distance makes him a citizen who reflects critically on politics, who derives his understanding of politics from the feeling of citizenship in his southern German home town and from the sources of European enlightenment.

Encounters with Reinhold Würth can be had on many stages of public life. However, when it comes to approaching him, the distances remain extensive. He has mastered the public appearance and knows how to shield himself from the intrusiveness that threatens everyone who enjoys media attention. He does not like the labels that are tacked onto him – "screw king," "tough cookie," to name only two examples – wherever something is written about him or one of his public appearances is announced. He only approached the attribute "founding father" with great reluctance too.

His affable style of friendly behaviour on his first encounters with strangers shrouds a reticence that preserves aloofness. In an instant, this can turn into a surprising experience of the ironic self-assurance that is inherent in the breed of people into which he was born. Today, he is still at home where he first saw the light of day: in Hohenlohe in the north of the German federal state of Baden-Württemberg, a region which is characterised by its citizens' head for business and the compartmentalised power structure of its aristocratic past. Where earldoms and principalities once dominated society, successful companies have now superseded the agricultural economic structure; many operate as world market leaders for highly specialised mechanical engineering on all continents.

He has revealed himself publicly as a liberal, he has made appearances during the election campaign of the FDP, the German liberal Free Democratic Party, he was a party member, but resigned out of disappointment about the party's own abandonment of its liberal brand essence. Reinhold Würth found one of his role models in Theodor Heuss, the first German President after the foundation of the Federal Republic of Germany out of the ruins of World War II. Würth sees the lack of political courage as a symptom of the decay of liberalism in Germany. This pains him grievously.

His vision of a United States of Europe stands against the backdrop of the economic and political power of China and the United States of America. His fear is that Europe could be squeezed between them. From his perspective, danger is also looming from the conflict between the West and Russia which has flared up because of Ukraine. For this reason, he has added his voice to a call by prominent German politicians and artists, including former German President Roman Herzog and the former head of the Federal Chancellery, Horst Teltschik; they are advocating a new German policy towards Russia on the basis of consideration of Moscow's reservations about a further territorial expansion by NATO and the EU.

In his political understanding, the distance to professional politics unites Reinhold Würth with most German entrepreneurs; they speak out about politics, support parties with donations for election campaigns, promote candidates – but never enter the ring of political battles themselves. As an entrepreneur, Reinhold Würth always remains mindful of his independence. He knows that active politics is another business.

He enjoys the freedom of the entrepreneur. Politics ruins business. This suspicion is the running theme when he points to the failures of politically motivated companies, political prestige projects and the failure of politicians who remain unsuccessful as managers in business.

The dialogues that are collected in this book emanated from the attempt to combine the lesser known sides of Reinhold Würth's personality with indepth insights into his motivations and the forces that stopped his vigour from flagging into a biblical age. None of this can be separated from the background of the story of the economic rise from a small screw shop in a backwater in Baden-Württemberg into a corporate group with global reach.

The ascent was not always straightforward for the entrepreneur, art collector, patron, family man and Christian. He speaks openly about how he handled failures, setbacks, disappointments and the extreme experiences against which wealth does not protect.

Autobiographical memories are blended with factual reports and narrative passages. It was never the intention to develop this book into a consecutive chronological life story that covered all phases and chapters of his life. The mere attempt to do this would be presumptuous in light of the dimensions of this entrepreneur's life and of his work. That project must remain reserved for the comprehensive biography of Reinhold Würth that is still outstanding. This will reveal, in the definition of the publicist Johannes Gross, a former joint editor of the Frankfurter Allgemeine Zeitung newspaper, a "classic rags-to-riches story" – "classic in the meaning of the American dream, but not typical of Europe."[1]

Because: "The ascent from the nothingness of generality to prestige, influence and success thanks to the achievements of only one generation was never commonplace on the Old Continent, only occurred from time to time in our century in the early years after World War II and is now becoming rarer again." What Johannes Gross wrote in the preface to a biography published in 1988 of Cologne entrepreneur Hans Imhoff can be quoted here with reference to Reinhold Würth, whose entrepreneurial success forms the axis around which everything in his life turns.

It was not committees, management boards or managers that made Germany into the land of the economic miracle after World War II. It was entrepreneurs, whose names we still remember even if their companies have foundered or fallen into the hands of others. They had little in common with regard to their personalities, their characters or their entrepreneurial fields of activity. But what unites them is their ambition and their power to make their company identical with themselves as if they belonged to a single guild.

When the death of entrepreneur Karl Albrecht, co-founder of the international trading company Aldi, became known in mid-July 2014, the Frankfurter Allgemeine Zeitung wrote in an obituary that he was the last founding father of German business. That is not correct. Reinhold Würth is also a founding father, in his company, in his family, in his entire personality. A founding father who resolutely champions European unity and at the same time professes his allegiance to his home (*Heimat*[2]) of Hohenlohe. He began his career as a commercial traveller and became a world traveller out of curiosity about discoveries. That is why he christened his yacht "Vibrant Curiosity."

In German post-war history, his name stands on a level with founders that became global players. Like Josef Schwarz (Lidl), Karl Albrecht (Aldi), Reinhard Mohn (Bertelsmann), Josef Neckermann and Max Grundig, he created a corporate group from a small firm. He is one of the last to have still experienced the Nazi dictatorship, World War II and its aftermath and then in the 1950s and 1960s to help shape the German economic miracle that still persists today. This generation of owners influences their companies throughout their lives, even if they have officially retired from active company management and handed over the reins to descendants or non-family managers.

Although he is on voyages of discovery on the "Vibrant Curiosity" for two or three months of the year, his presence in the company is permanence. The seeds of criticism tend to burgeon particularly with regard to the company's orientation towards the founding father. Who dares to contradict him? From whom does he accept objections? The loneliness of power applies to entrepreneurs too.

It is rumoured both inside and outside the company – usually only in confidence – that he brooks no management to emerge beside or below, not to mention above him, even if he has officially retired from management. This is a sensitive issue – and he does not shy away from it on the pages of this book. Likewise the tax affair that affected him deeply. Even today, his bitterness about it has not dissipated. When he introduces a speech to the press club in Stuttgart with the statement: "You have here before you a convicted tax criminal," then the self-deprecation is only a façade behind which the wound aches.

He is delighted with his awards for his patronage of the arts, the recognition of his philanthropic commitment, the distinctions for his sponsorship of academic projects. He has received several honorary doctorates and an honorary professorship. The captain of his yacht, a British man, calls him "the professor." In his family they say: "our father;" one grandson calls him by his first name.

The titles and epithets mark his central living spaces: the Würth Group, the ownership with the social obligation required in the Basic Law (the German constitution) to which Reinhold Würth shows his commitment through his actions, the cultural scenes he likes to move in, the universities which he hopes will provide elite education for Germany's future, the family where Reinhold Würth feels at home.

Würth created a global trading group that is based on one idea: the idea that screws are more than metal pins with threads that keep parts of a whole together. In the same way that letters form the communication system of writing, he made the screw into one element in a system category – the fastening system. It offers a multiplication of the goods that are tradable in the system, of which screws are only one. This concept mirrors the holistic thought process that Reinhold Würth practices, and maybe also a penchant for the tinkering that caused him to make a device to accelerate screwing processes from an old sewing machine when he was still a boy.

Germany has achieved worldwide recognition and esteem as an imaginative manufacturer of industrial goods like cars or machine tools. The

Germans were never known as a nation of traders. Even today, trade is still associated more with the Mediterranean character. Trade was traditionally associated with seafaring and access to the sea. The successful traders in Germany operated in Hamburg, Bremen, Lübeck – at best anywhere that navigable rivers ran to the sea.

Würth started out as a trader on the small, non-navigable River Kocher that ends in the Neckar, and thus does not even run into the sea indirectly. One of his favourite stories from the start of his career tells how he delivered the packages in which customers received the screws, nuts and washers they had ordered with a handcart. His first car was a VW Beetle. That enabled him to extend his radius of activity to the whole of Germany.

He appends another story: One day, he wanted to be able to reach more customers than was possible with a car. He drove to Stuttgart and bought his first plane, a single-engine Cessna. At that time, however, he was not yet able to fly. He knew a few people in the flying school: "You have to teach me how to fly." Now he could serve customers in the Rhineland, in Westphalia and in Hamburg in one day from the grass runway in Schwäbisch Hall, be home again in the evening and enter the results into his sales books. He is overcome by nostalgic joy when he tells about this.

Even today, he still states his profession as commercial traveller. I flew to China with him from the Adolf Würth Airport in Schwäbisch Hall, which was named after his father and belongs to the Group. He sat in the cockpit of the three-engine Falcon throughout the night – on the left, in the pilot's seat. Arrival in Shenzhen at five in the morning. At ten a.m. RW, as he is called internally in Künzelsau, was sitting in the conference room with the Chinese delegation – wide-awake, because this was about business.

Anyone who seeks the roots of Würth's success here will find them. Würth calls selling the nicest profession in the world. That sounds like window-dressing for a trivial business, but Würth turned it into the model of a passion for travelling and dealing with people and products. He requires this commitment of the salespeople in the Group – sometimes in letters in which the founding father demands increased performance in a way that is released into the public domain and appears in "Der Spiegel" news magazine as wielding the whip. And he himself appears in "Manager Magazin" as a tough cookie.

Würth values achievement as an implicit prerequisite for self-fulfilment in life. It seems reasonable to discern in this a reflection of his origins in the Württemberg backwaters, where piety was combined with the natural frugality of life. In his curriculum vitae, we encounter the image of the Protestant as described by sociologist Max Weber with a "a special tendency to develop economic rationalism," albeit without the ascetic trait that the protagonist of the Protestant ethos attributes to him.[3]

Würth knows how to practice joie de vivre and enjoyment of life. He allows the Group and his employees to participate in this when there are anniversaries of the company and its founder to be celebrated. He enjoys his wealth, the beauty of his homes in Hermersberg and Salzburg, the elegance of his yacht. Yet he nurtures characteristics that are far removed from showing off. Because he does not flaunt anything, he keeps his distance from the glossy world that is a meeting place for all those who like to see themselves on the pages of the society magazines. He has also maintained a modicum of puritanism in his enjoyment of life. That makes it easier for him to postulate modesty as a virtue for himself and for others, even in wealth.

No other company in Europe employs as many permanent salespeople as the Würth Group: more than 30,000. The Group is a complex selling machine, comprising more than 400 individual and affiliated companies. The Group has achieved the size that sustains its own hotels and restaurants, its own event agency with travel agent and a publishing house. Like the company's own airport in Schwäbisch Hall, where in Nazi times the first German fighter jets operated and which the American occupation forces later used for their liaison aircraft take-offs and landings, many of the Group's other service divisions are also used by companies that are not part of the Group. This is consistent with Würth's business approach: Entrepreneurial activity must be profit-oriented.

Even as an art collector, he is not unaffected by this. "I am still a businessman, even when I collect art," he admits publicly. The art collection and its central inventories belong to the Group or to individual Group companies. It is a connecting link between the working environment and the educational function that in Würth's view is inherent in the origins of art: inspiring people, giving them bearings to find meaning in their lives above and beyond day-to-day concerns. In our dialogues, it was clear time and again how much this idea guides the entrepreneur and collector.

In the broad expanse of his activities, the qualities of a hedonist do not remain concealed. The book that will be published to mark his 80th birthday can only reveal in a rudimentary fashion the multi-faceted nature of this great entrepreneurial personality. The reader is given the possibility to approach Reinhold Würth in a way that leads to immense respect for his life's work.

Comments

1 Hans-Josef Joest: Auf der Schokoladenseite. Hans Imhoff – eine Nachkriegskarriere. [On the Chocolaty Side. Hans Imhoff – a Post-War Career] Düsseldorf, Vienna, New York 1988, p. 10.
2 The German word "Heimat" is a concept describing one's place of origin or acquired affinity, evoking emotional ties and a sense of belonging.
3 Max Weber: The Protestant Ethic and the Spirit of Capitalism. Cologne 2009, p. 7.

Chapter 1:
The founding father makes provisions

The family will retain the management

A set of rules is binding to shareholders and management / Power is transferred to the Advisory Board / The Trust Council supports the transition / The worlds of art and work remain united

> *You have made provisions for the company management after your time. In light of the size of the Group and the high profile you yourself have, that is not a purely private issue.*

I make no secret of it. We are a corporate group with a transparent structure; we publish our annual report every year from which the ownership structure can be derived. The Group is owned by family trusts that are managed by family members and non-family people.

The settlement of my succession, the safeguarding of both the organisation and the structural foundations of the Würth Group after my death and the provisions for my family, did not just start to occupy my mind since I began to approach my 80th birthday, when I would enter a Biblical age. I can well remember how I sat on the bed fine-tuning the text of my will on the evening of 18 March, 1985 in the Seagull Hotel in Shanghai while on a trip to the Far East. That was shortly before my 50th birthday.

I have always been aware of the responsibility I have for the company, for its employees and for the preservation of its economic and organisational foundations. Since my youth I was accustomed to taking on responsibility. When my father died unexpectedly in 1954, I was 19 years old. Then I was suddenly the boss, supported by my mother. I was more or less automatically given the duty and responsibility. That was simply necessary. Yet it was not even my mother's ideal. She would have liked to see me become a teacher.

> *But in 1985 in Shanghai you weren't toying with the idea of handing over management of the business?*

No. That was a precautionary measure. At that time, the Würth Group already had almost 8,000 employees. And I had a young family. I could not leave it to chance or to unknown lawyers to decide what should happen if something were to befall me. I had to make provisions for the business as well as for the private areas of my life in the event of my death. That was how I viewed my responsibility even back then.

> But you had already made several attempts to surrender operational management before you handed over the chair of the Advisory Board to your daughter Bettina. Do you find it hard to let go?

Internally, for your entire life, you will never be able to completely shake off the responsibility for a company that you built up yourself and that is as big as the Würth Group is today; you cannot just take it off like a coat at the theatre cloakroom. That is the mental side. Maybe I have to admit that the previous Chairman of the Central Managing Board was right when he held a mirror quite close to my face once and said that an entrepreneur like me could "not renounce overnight the entrepreneurial playing field, the facets of his power and the experience in order to drive the company forward."

> It is your declared intention to create stability for the future of the Group in its existence and its management through the family trusts that were established in 1987. Doubts are being voiced about the success of this model by pointing to examples of other family-owned companies. Did you not consider company preservation trusts like Bosch, ZF or Mahle as models?

Each entrepreneur has to find the solution that he deems to be the most suitable for himself, for his company and for his family. There is no model that applies to everyone. Each individual initial situation must be regarded separately from the others. The company, the entrepreneur, the family situation and tradition, the capital structure and the market conditions are so different that you cannot say: This or that is a solution that applies to everyone, it is the right or ideal solution. But there is one thing that all owner-entrepreneurs have in common: their responsibility for what they have created, for the company, for the family, for the employees' jobs.

There are three types of trusts: charitable trusts, company preservation trusts and family trusts. I deliberately chose the family trust model because I want to preserve the assets in the family. The doubts about this model can be countered with positive examples from other family-owned companies.

The Zeiss, Mahle or Bosch models are not what I envisage for my family. It will retain the ownership. We have agreements and obligations for the legacy with which we have arranged the management structure, the management methods and the decision-making processes in a way that, from today's perspective, will prevent the family from degenerating into opposing camps and the Group into splintered parts. The charitable side is reflected in the charitable Würth trust. This trust is financed by Group companies, and I believe that this has proven itself well.

It was important to me right from the start to prevent what I have read all too often in the press and have seen confirmed in my life experience. That is, that entire families start to fight in inheritance cases, become enemies one against the other, that deals are made that last for generations, and that families often only ever meet in court. Then energies are expended on the battles of the clans instead of on the market and on the company. I wanted to spare my family this by any means possible.

I also did not want to leave the Group to the mercy of the randomness of family developments. My vision is that the Würth Group can continue to be run and developed as a family-owned firm.

Life experience shows how healthy and prosperous family-owned companies have to be sold in the second, third or fourth generation, and only because one element of the heirs regards the firm as a cash cow, or wants to cash in on it, sometimes out of short-sighted self-interest.

This is why I developed the solution of the family trusts, put the entire fortune into the family trusts and thus indicated to the family: You will never get your hands on the physical assets. You cannot fight about whether someone got too much or too little. The fortune has been isolated from the family in the trusts. That is a huge asset.

I have even made contracts with both my daughters about relinquishing statutory shares. That was important for the first ten years after the trusts were set up, if something should have happened to me. At that time, my daughters would at least have been able to assert their right to statutory shares. That in turn could have endangered corporate value. Today, that no longer has any relevance, because the ten years have long since passed. The problem of the statutory shares has solved itself.

Of course, another concern of mine was to provide well for my family. I want to be a good father, grandfather, great-grandfather. I was able to fulfil this wish well in the trust's statutes. The family members are beneficiaries of the trusts. As Chairman of the Supervisory Board of the Würth Group's Family Trusts, I agree the annual beneficiary payments with the family members, which are then passed by resolution by the five-member Supervisory Board.

With respect to the management, I created the Advisory Board. The Advisory Board has very precisely elaborated statutes. They define who can be a member of the Advisory Board; age limits have been set. The Advisory Board has nine members. Five are appointed by the family. The Advisory Board has the task of advising and monitoring the managing directors of the Würth Group. It decides on the appointment and removal of the managing directors of the companies in the Würth Group.

> *Regardless of all internal arrangements – outwardly you are still the undisputed founding father, who by his mere presence as a person has a defining and integrating effect.*

So, let us move on to my succession now. From my perspective, I have plainly taken a back seat. Maybe it has not really been noticed yet. We know this from almost every area of our lives: Changes in society often take years before the public is aware of them. Likewise, looking at the Würth Group – whether from an internal or an external perspective – you need time before the light bulb goes on: The old guy is no longer right at the top of the pile at all now.

> *It is hard to imagine that you do not intervene when in doubt. You are the Chairman of the Supervisory Board – don't you have the last word in all important affairs merely by virtue of this fact?*

All decisions that are important for the company are played out in a clear structure where the competencies, tasks, appointments and removals are stipulated. We have a set of rules and regulations for this that we call our compendium. It could also be called the Würth Group rule book. It includes the family, who has transferred its rights as equity owners to the family trusts. The family decides on three of the five seats on the Supervisory Board and five of the nine seats on the Advisory Board of the Würth Group according to established rules. Hence members that do not belong to the family are included in both bodies. They are appointed according to the rules stipulated in the compendium. On the Supervisory Board, one family seat each comes from the lines of my daughter Marion and my daughter Bettina, they have to appoint the third one together. If they cannot find a solution, that is carried out by the head of the Higher Regional Court in Stuttgart. The Supervisory Board is at the top of the hierarchy, followed by the Advisory Board, which supervises business transactions like a supervisory board and decides on budgets and investments. Operational management is carried out by the Central Managing Board and the management of the operational units. The non-family members of the Supervisory Board and Advisory Board have been designated by me in my will and will co-opt their successors themselves later.

How much power – in a formal sense too – have you retained?

While I am alive, I will retain rights that will no longer exist in that form after my time. This has proven itself during the arrangement of all the provisions for the time after my time. Even 28 years ago when we set up the family trusts, I imagined that one day I would see – as an observer, so to speak – how the company developed further after me and without me. However, I wanted to still be able to make adjustments. Thus there was a clear wish: The company will leave my hands – or more precisely, I will leave the centre of the company. However, I wanted to still be able to intervene here and there. And that actually did occur like that in practice.

I developed the compendium about the legal structure of the Würth Group that I mentioned earlier together with notaries, business lawyers, financial experts, etc. Everything was discussed extensively and then adopted. Despite all the diligence and competence of the participants, the odd loophole in the text did emerge in the course of the years. Then I could still intervene at that stage.

Let me give you an example: Highly precise regulations are foreseen for the disposal of company shareholdings or the incorporation of shareholdings etc. However, not a word was mentioned about leasing companies. That means, this loophole could have been used and Adolf Würth KG could have been leased to God knows whom, along with its entire active business operations. You could have said: It isn't expressly forbidden, after all. After discovering this loophole, I had the regulation incorporated that the leasing of companies or parts of companies was subject to the approval of the Advisory Board and the Supervisory Boards. For smaller volumes, the decision of the Advisory Board is sufficient; but when the volumes are larger, then heavy demands are placed on the Supervisory Board too and it is also responsible.

Theoretically, the company can also be sold or converted into a joint-stock company. In those cases, the unanimous vote of the Supervisory Board is required. Thus the non-family members must also be in agreement on such a serious decision. However, the Supervisory Board members who do not belong to the family are not obliged first and foremost to the wellbeing of the family, but to the company and its employees to the same extent. I believe that this is an even balance of power that ultimately always leads to sensible solutions.

Likewise, an important experience from the criminal tax proceedings induced me to make a change to the compendium. Initially, no majority of seats was foreseen for the family on the Supervisory Board and on the Advisory Board. Then the experiences with external advisors in my tax dispute prompted me to secure the power for the family in the two most important bodies.

> *Your daughter Bettina Würth is Chairwoman of the Advisory Board. However, she is overshadowed by your strong presence in the company and in the public eye.*

That may appear that way outwardly. Internally, my daughter is a real presence in the company. Last week, we had our staff meeting for Adolf Würth KG. It was led on the stage by the Chairwoman of the Advisory Board together with the Chairman of the Central Managing Board, Mr Friedmann, and with Mr Zürn. Thus we experience in practice that she holds the chair of the Advisory Board and hence is the number one in the Group.

On this occasion, we also celebrated the fact that Bettina has been with the company for 30 years.

> *The Trust Council is a unique feature of the Würth Group. There is no works council. However, elsewhere in our dialogues you emphasised that you are not fundamentally against works councils. How is the Trust Council behaving in the transition phase where management passes from you to your daughter?*

The Trust Council also views the transition process favourably. It values the fact that the family is at the head of the company in the next generation. The knowledge of being in a family-owned company gives the employees security. They know that we will not sell and thus that their jobs have a high level of security.

> *How does the Trust Council work?*

It is a highly democratic process. We hold Trust Council elections every four years. The 27 members come from all areas, from among the sales reps, from the warehouse, commercial administration, etc. There are always around twice as many candidates, or sometimes even more, than are elected. A secret ballot is held, and votes are counted before witnesses. Thus this Trust Council is constituted as a democratic body. Only with the difference that we do not, as stipulated in the Works Constitution Act for works councils, release a certain number of people from duty. The members of the Trust Council continue to work at their normal workstations, but are always available whenever someone has difficulties or problems.

Let me give you an example: This morning, I led a meeting with around 25 employees from the most diverse business areas at Würth KG. No one from the management was there – but the Trust Council Chairman was.

Every year, we hold a big staff meeting that is organised by the Trust Council. The Chairman of the Trust Council opens this event. There are almost 2,000 people in the room. The management reports on how business is going and so on, like the management board does in other companies in a works council meeting or a staff meeting.

All the wage negotiations, company agreements about Christmas bonuses and holiday bonuses – they are all handled and negotiated with the Trust Council. Then there are works agreements on it.

> *Are they similar to a collective bargaining agreement in form and content?*

For decades it has been our tradition to adhere relatively precisely to the collective bargaining agreement of IG Metall, the German metalworkers' union. If there is a wage increase in it, we follow it comprehensively. That is certainly the answer to the question of why we don't have a works council: Based on our type of business, which is a trading company in its primary focus, we actually belong in the realm of the former Trading, Banking and Insurance Trade Union (HBV), which is now Verdi. Hourly wages are lower there than in the IG Metall agreements. So if the requirement came that we should form a works council to conform completely to the law, then the employees can have one – but with the consequence of three years of horizontal pay freeze, until the level of the Verdi wage agreement has been reached, which IG Metall already has. So the people would gain themselves a dramatic disadvantage for a period of three years if they wanted a works council. That is possibly a brake that explains why it is not done.

If you went to a Trust Council meeting today and did not know that this is our Trust Council, you would not notice at all that it is not a works council. Confrontational negotiations and discussions take place there. We just have the huge advantage that we don't have everyone waving around the Works Constitution Act – neither the Trust Council, nor the management. We can settle most things quickly and informally by consensus.

> *But even trusting and reliable cooperation between external management and the family as owners requires regular practice that has to be translated into practical experience on both sides. Have you set guidelines for this?*

The guidelines are set down in the compendium I already mentioned. It does not just determine the legal structure. It establishes rules ranging from the investment plan through corporate planning up to procedures in key personnel issues. These are all issues that have to be approved by the

Advisory Board. It is the same in other companies. It is put into practice in our company in this way with my daughter at the forefront. The Advisory Board is very active and sometimes very, very critical.

> *Can it be said that the power that was concentrated in your presence in the company is now shifting into the Advisory Board?*

Yes, of course. Into the Advisory Board and the Supervisory Board. If I die today, nothing much will happen. And nothing at all in the legal structure. Nor will inheritance tax be incurred to such an extent that the family has to sell off anything. That has all been dealt with already. In 2010, I instigated an early inheritance for the trusts so that they have peace for 30 years – until 2040. None of us can know what will happen then.

What is important is this: If it comes down to it, the management and the supervisory bodies are fully functional and ever-present, they work in strict adherence to the set of rules and regulations. We have three Advisory Board meetings a year. If an unscheduled opportunity somehow arises to acquire a company, then a decision has to be made rapidly. In such cases, a decision is taken by the Advisory Board by written consent in lieu of a meeting. It has happened maybe on two or three occasions that an extraordinary meeting had to be called. That was the case when we acquired Uni-Elektro, the big electrical wholesaler.

We are currently working on an acquisition that I would like to make. In these cases, I need the Advisory Board too. The Board had acted so tentatively on my first attempt that I withdrew the motion. I was effectively outvoted. However, I continued to work on the project and refined the decision basis. It was not until the second attempt that I succeeded in gaining the Advisory Board's approval.

I do not wish to and cannot afford to pass over the Advisory Board. I adhere to the rules that I established myself. I do not want to add another example to the list of family-owned companies where advisory bodies resigned. That would be more than embarrassing to me if something like that appeared in the press about us. So: The Advisory Board has power which it also very definitely exerts and which I respect. Of course, that is not quite so visible in the public eye.

> *In the public eye, the dominant image is: There is Mr Würth, and he does whatever he likes…*

That is not true at all.

> *Outwardly, you are Würth and Würth is you…*

That is purely the result of the art activities. I certainly assume that even after my time the company will maintain and enhance its good reputation from this combination of affinity to the fine arts and company vision. This engenders a level of appeal in the public eye that must be nurtured. After all, it is not just a hobby of mine. We are doing something for the society in which and with which we live and do business. I see it as a philanthropic act – but also as a benefit for our company.

> *You once said at the opening of an exhibition that you were also a businessman when you were purchasing art.*

I have a smaller private art collection. But most of the works in the Würth collection belong to the company and are thus part of the company assets. This is in keeping with our philosophy to make our workplaces into places with cultural influence too. We have connected our workplace to the world of art. Our employees experience art at their workplaces. And we make our art collection accessible to the public in the forums and museums. That is part of our corporate culture.

> *Every year, tens of thousands of visitors experience the enjoyment of the fine arts in these forums and museums. The Würth brand is influenced to a high degree by art collector Würth in person. And also by the identification of the collector with the museums and forums, which has an effect in the public eye. Will that remain your individual legacy in the sense of an obligation that goes beyond your time?*

You could say that. It will also remain a duty for the family to maintain it like this. That is a strong commitment. Wherever we do business with our companies, we promote the regional culture there. We bring world culture to the regions. That is a characteristic of the Würth corporate culture. It is philanthropic, but also positive for the companies' positioning in their markets. You can definitely say: The pleasure I take in collecting art has never harmed business. It promotes the level of appeal among the public. Of course, this should be cultivated in the future too.

> You have a model that is essentially different from the procedures of other large collections, like for example Marx in Berlin or Sprengel in Hanover. You have no foundations that unite your collections with public-sector museums. Why did you take another path?

The art collection is explicitly company property and it is intended to stay that way too. I did that deliberately because I want to maintain the value of the art collection in the company as liable equity. The acquisitions are financed from company funds. The museums are on company premises and are interconnected with the companies. That will stay that way after my time too. It is not a contradiction in terms to view the acquisition of art works under the aspect of their material value too.

I see our corporate philosophy here too. We work in an ambience of culture. For that reason alone it would be fatal if someone were to tear it apart. No one can afford to do that.

> At the moment, you decide on the acquisitions. You set the tone. Without you, the Holbein Madonna would not have moved from the Schirn gallery in Frankfurt am Main to the Johanniterkirche church in Schwäbisch Hall. What will happen to the continuity?

The Chairwoman of the Advisory Board, my daughter Bettina, is a member of our Art Advisory Board. I could envisage that at some stage my granddaughter Maria would be able to take over management of the collection, which is currently held by our director, Sylvia Weber. Maria is studying history of art. Bettina has an affinity to art, she collects artworks. She has acquired an entire range of artists that are also present in the company collection.

> Will authority pass from you to the Art Advisory Board?

The Art Advisory Board has authority – even now. It meets regularly. I was in Karlsruhe a few days ago, visited visual artists and bought artworks too. Those are the smaller things that I decide without the Advisory Board.

But when it is a matter of substantial things, for example works that cost €500,000 or more – then I act only with the approval of the Art Advisory Board as a matter of principle. I could do that myself too, but it is also to a certain degree confirmation for me that the decision is correct. I am a businessman even when I buy art. But I have to say I have never observed such variance in a supervisory body anywhere like on this Art Advisory Board. Artists are artists, and it is very rare that there is ever a unanimous decision.

> *In Greek antiquity, Zeus pops up time and again as the ubiquitous being. Zeus, who regularly goes down into the world and makes sure everything is running properly. Are you following the Zeus model by regularly showing your presence in your companies around the world?*

What do you mean by that? You surely don't want to compare me to Zeus, do you?

> *Are you not seen sometimes in a comparable role? Even in your 80th year, you still identify with your company. You contribute your drive and your energy to the Group every day. Let us not stretch the god comparison any further. Can you see yourself better reflected in the image of the founding father?*

That depends on the image you hold up to me. Do you just want me to look in the mirror? Or what image do you have in your mind of a founding father?

> *Let me take a description that I find applicable from the book "Die Psyche des Patriarchen" (The Psyche of the Founding Father) which has also been published by Frankfurter Allgemeine Buch. In that book, the founding father of the company is defined as a father figure according to the archetype of the family patriarch. He holds the reins, ensures that his instructions are carried out consistently and, despite all his severity, displays a fatherly lenience and forbearance in his actions, and always sees the entire person when he is judging his employees.*

I do not follow a stereotypical pattern. And I won't let myself be shoehorned into it either. My understanding of my role as entrepreneur is related to my understanding of responsibility. If you understand me as a founding father because of my responsibility, I will not contradict that.

After all, there are 66,000 jobs that have to be safeguarded and made sustainable. In addition, living with the company is quite simply enjoyable. I have sometimes said that the company is my electric train set. Not that I see the company as a toy, but a company can also exert the same fascination on adults that I felt as a child when two or three trains ran on the track system without crashing into each other, if that is understood as a large feat of collaboration of many people in a well-functioning organisation.

We are a company with many facets. In a certain sense, we have become a conglomerate. We do not specialise in assembly and fastening material alone. A few days ago, we inaugurated the new Würth Elektronik building in Waldzimmern. The Group has entirely different dimensions than it used to have, when it was stuck in a certain one-dimensionality. Today, there is much more emphasis on technology, materials physics and chemistry than there used to be. As a businessman, I do not have very much say in that. Today, we have become a flowery conglomerate. If everything interacts well, if a good operating result comes out and the company has a great balance sheet, then it is simply beautiful.

> *Does it bother you when you are still called the screw king in the media?*

You become thick-skinned too! At the beginning, I certainly did get really annoyed about such a stupid expression. But you can't make it go away; so you just have to accept it.

> *An economic scientist said: No one is born an entrepreneur, that is to say, a founding father, but grows into the role in a complex process. Do you agree?*

Yes, you grow into the role. Whether that is a complex process I don't know. It basically occurs automatically. It is like as if you would say: A tree grows bigger in a complex system. The tree simply grows towards the light of its own accord.

But only if it has the intrinsic gene that is required for it to do so. Another quote: "Direct contact to workers and employees is very important to a founding father."

Excuse me. I do not like the differentiation between workers and employees. That stems from another era. I speak about employees.

Employees then. I had not reached the end of the quote. This contact with the employees "assumes the constant presence of the founding father."

I am not constantly present. I am away for two to three months a year – travelling.

But even when you are travelling, you exert a constant presence through your letters. That has a fascinating, almost anachronistic component. The letter writer is becoming increasingly rare nowadays. Today people send mails and post on Twitter for all their worth. Governing by letter is going out of fashion.

Yes, that is true. I am attached to paper, although I use the new communication methods myself – selectively and specifically.

Do you write notes by hand?

I have dictating machines. I never write any notes for myself. I dictate, if possible ready to be typed up. Sometimes a type of diary. But always letters, every day.

How many thousands or hundreds of thousands of letters have you written to date?

We are up in the region of 150,000 at the moment. All letters are numbered consecutively. I no longer know when we began doing that. Maybe my secretaries know this.

> That could become a little book in its own right: *Management by Letters.*

I have learned this as life experience: It is immensely important to write things down. That started very simply. Employees came along who claimed that they had been promised a higher salary or a larger car. However, I could not recall any such promises. It was then that I introduced a system where I set out all important things in writing in letters. Because everything that is in writing is verifiable and has validity. Since then, I have had peace from – well, let us just say, misunderstandings. I no longer have problems of people coming and saying to me: You promised me this or that. Having things in writing creates order, maintains peace and quiet and harmony. That is why I never want to do without the letter format, even in times of mails and Twitter and Facebook and all those other things.

> That has something to do with our life experience, with our age. But do the younger people adopt it too? Younger people find it very hard to write letters at all anymore.

They have to answer my letters, after all. In 80 percent of my letters, there is a text at the bottom saying: Answer requested by a certain date. Depending on the problem, I give them up to two weeks to respond.

> And you expect a response by letter, not by email?

If necessary, I will also accept an email nowadays. But I prefer to get a nice letter, with letterhead and signature. It does not have to be as elaborate as it used to be in the nineteenth century.

We have a large company archive. Recently, I viewed old bookkeeping documents at our subsidiary Arnold Umformtechnik – the company is 117 years old. It is a feast for the eyes when you look at these invoice forms from 1898 and 1919! A third of a DIN A4 page has just the letterhead, the company name written beautifully in a semicircle and underneath a picture of the company premises. A lovingly designed page from bookkeeping tells something about the company. Where do you find something like this nowadays? Or that aesthetic of handwriting in the business correspondence of former times?

> There is an underlying nostalgia there that is a constant temptation for our generation.

I am pragmatic. In a company, there is no going back to inkwell and quill. If I cannot attend an important event at the company, I often make a video which is then played on the occasion in question. That also contributes to the impression that I have a high presence.

> Thus it will be all the more noticeable when your personal presence is no longer possible, because your life is coming to a close. There are no video messages from the hereafter.

There is what you leave behind. I do not mean the material things. I mean the principles that have been lived in a company, for which employees have been gained, which were recognised internally and externally, which proved themselves and thus continue to exist. At least, that is what I would hope for. This gives that which I understand under the heading of responsibility a timeless dimension that goes beyond me. It is also part of entrepreneurial responsibility to impart principles that are permanently valid and practicable in such a way that they can be effective beyond one's own lifetime. We have such principles. Everyone can read them on the internet.

> These principles are very wide-ranging – from the admonition to always make a profit with the company right up to the etiquette rule that requires friendly interaction with one another. What binding force do these guidelines you are leaving behind have?

A company is not an educational organisation. It is a living organism that develops and changes. The principles which we have encapsulated into our corporate philosophy bind all structures and employees to values by which we want to and should be guided in our work. They are standards, so to speak, for self-examination and self-reassurance. The corporate philosophy is binding company law for all Group companies in Germany and abroad. This is stipulated in the compendium I mentioned.

There is an example in the principles: The management of the Würth Group is not geared to authoritarian leadership, but cooperation. But beside this it is also stated clearly that the management, in its responsibility for the preservation and the safeguarding of the existence of the Würth

Group, has to make the final decision following a cooperative process of opinion-making.

Another example: We practice decentralised management in all areas. But: Anyone who is unsuccessful has to relinquish responsibilities. Our success orientation follows the commandment: "The bigger the success, the bigger the degree of freedom."

No matter how important the rules for interpersonal etiquette which we want to practice in our company might be, life experience teaches us that elementary principles are all too easily forgotten if they are not constantly called to mind. That is why I marked the starting position for economic success clearly. One could also call that a regulatory orientation.

Although it sounds self-evident, it is written in a preamble that precedes the principles that every company must generate profit. That is formulated and justified very clearly: "The achievement-oriented society of the Western world compels the deployment of the factors of labour, capital and raw materials where the highest yields can be expected. The success of our economic rise since then is inextricably linked to this ideology." This portrays the basis for how we do business.

This is also specified with regard to the time after me: "Enhancing profitability and increasing profit will remain top priority for every activity in the Würth Group in the future too. New funds for investments can only be provided and the growth of our Group can only be safeguarded through the company profit. Growth without profit is lethal." Although this is not written explicitly in our guidelines: I agree with Swiss entrepreneur Nicolas Hayek, who said: "It is not the big ones who eat the small ones, but the fast ones that eat the slow ones."

We also describe our regulatory self-image in a pluralist, that is to say liberal society: "The Würth Group feels a commitment to the principle of a free democratic civil society and to the social market economy."

I have always seen myself as part of civil society. I would like to pass this on to the family. That is why it is written in the compendium as my wish for heirs and successors that they act "as industrious and upright citizens" for the good of the entire family and of the company and "feel attached to the good of the community in the sense of the social obligation of ownership."

How much pride is involved when you now, in your eightieth year, see the results of your life's achievement increasingly passing into the hands of others?

I would be lying if I did not admit that I am a little proud of what has emerged. But at the same time I am of course aware that I could have never done that alone. The success of the Würth Group has many fathers. I am certainly always dependent on each and every employee and feel that way too. But the other side of the coin is that this company, with its 66,000 employees, would have probably never come about if it was not for me. I claim the right to say that I myself directly or indirectly employed most of these industrious men and women who are working in management positions in the Group today.

You could devote yourself entirely to art, discover the last corners of the Earth that you don't know yet with your yacht, practice contemplation, read what you have always wanted to read in your library – but you do nothing of the sort. What energy drives you to devote yourself untiringly to the company in the eightieth year of your life?

I would like to leave everything behind in top condition when I have to make my last exit.

WÜRTH GROUP

The Guidelines

Our vision

Becoming the number 1 in the eyes of our customers
As the best sales team.

What spurs us on

We love selling.
We inspire our customers.

Our principles

We demand and promote performance.
The bigger the success,
the bigger the degree of freedom.

We are optimistic, dynamic and
have strong powers of self-assertion.

We fight passionately for success.

We consistently pursue everything
that has proven to be successful, and
we try out new things.

We strive for perfection in everything we do.

We assume responsibility for our actions,
work in mutual respect and are straightforward
and predictable in everything we do.

The most important word in our dealings
with one another is "thank you".

(The guidelines are published on the Würth Group website and are on view in displays in the company.)

Chapter 2
In a world that has come off the rails

The businessman has to know what is happening in politics

Call for a new policy on Russia / War is looming over Europe again / Peace zone from Lisbon to Vladivostok

> *By nature you are not what the Anglo-Saxons call a "political animal." Yet there are trenchant statements from you about politics. In response to recent events you took a critical stand on Berlin's foreign policy. What brings you to politics?*

As a businessman I have to know what is happening in politics. Because the Würth Group does not do its business in Germany alone, but around the world, I have to get my bearings about political developments on a global scale. To be honest, the inefficiency of politics annoys me – not just German politics; one can get annoyed about how politics across the world runs at idle, where urgent problems stay unsolved. As a liberal citizen, I also know that people make it too easy for themselves when they simply rail against politics and politicians. I must recognise that as a citizen I not only have a right to speak out; as a citizen, I also have a responsibility for our state. If one takes this responsibility seriously, one must stand up when something goes wrong.

> *You are one of the Western critics who have called for another policy towards Russia. What caused you to subscribe to this appeal, whose signatories include former German President Roman Herzog and former Development Minister Erhard Eppler?*

After the collapse of the Soviet Union, we all just hoped that the Cold War in Europe would be replaced by a blueprint for a lasting peace into which Russia was incorporated. But no new order emerged. Instead, armed conflicts are flaring up in Europe on the edges of the former Soviet Union. I find that the policy the West pursued towards Russia was wrong. The vision of a huge European free trade zone from Lisbon to Vladivostok has yielded to a hot conflict with Russia. That is why the central concern of this appeal is to bring about a new policy towards Russia. The call clearly shows the threat of war that is emerging from the Ukraine crisis. The danger that a hot war could come about between Russia and the European Union along with the United States is being underestimated.

We have not sufficiently realised that the world has come off the rails. In this analysis, I refer to the former U.S. Secretary of State Henry Kissinger, who bemoans the lack of a new world order in his latest book. He regards Europe as unable to cope with its responsibility in international politics and fears that a time is impending that is dictated by forces which are no longer limited by any order. He perceives a discrepancy between the technologically unlimited, global communication ability and growing information deficits between states and nations.

In the Ukraine conflict, Vladimir Putin is being incriminated as the incarnation of evil. All the blame is being laid on him, irrespective of whether this is objectively correct or not. Here in Germany, too, biased propaganda is being practiced and the normal citizen is being programmed, so to speak. Our call was kept quiet in the top news on our television stations or at best mentioned in passing. We discussed this in our dialogue about the media.

Let us go back to the Fall of the Iron Curtain – at that time, Russia had been promised that NATO would not expand eastward. And what did they do? They admitted Poland, Lithuania, Latvia and Estonia. A sphere of influence was assumed into the West from Russia. It must be understood that from a Russian viewpoint, this can engender fears about one's own position. That is a breach of promise by the West, and in that respect we have no call to put on airs as saints here. We are actively involved in this conflict too. Our politicians travelled to the Maidan Square in Kiev, made promises that they are unable to honour now. The Russians justifiably reproach us because the government in Kiev, which the West is supporting, came to power through a coup.

> *Those who advocate a hard line towards Russia cast you into the Putin sympathisers' box because of this position. Does that not bother you?*

Why should it? I form my own opinion and do not let myself be shoehorned into a corner where they would like to see me. In this respect I am like my grandfather. I follow his maxim: Do what is right and don't shy away from anyone!

> On many occasions, you have spoken about the friendliness of the Russian people, saying it is given too little consideration here in Germany and recedes behind the Putin image. Where do you get these impressions from? Is our image of Russia drawn by the wrong people?

Of course. Let me give you an example. In Salzburg, many people only see those Russians who flaunt their money and take a bar apart, start a brawl or shout loudly. This is how a misleading negative impression of Russians comes about.

However, anyone like my wife and myself too, who got to know Russia from many trips from St. Petersburg via Irkutsk to Kamchatka, comes to the conclusion: There are few other places in the world where I experience so many warm-hearted people. Most Russians are good and hospitable people, helpful, xenophile. Even towards us Germans, although we perpetrated bad things in Russia. It can also be seen in this: Those who travel little, who do not leave their village and only follow the media, they usually have completely wrong ideas. The quicker they come out, the more they travel, the broader their horizon will be and the better also their understanding toward others.

And that is why we say: If we want to advance Europe without a permanent conflict with Russia, a very important component is the promotion of mutual acquaintance, of growing together, of building together – including through tourism.

> Is the allegiance to the West still a guarantee for our security under current conditions and thus also for our business activities?

It is quite clear that we are friends of the United States in our security policy and will remain so in future too. And of course indirectly via NATO too. Our security policy interests are in the best hands in the Western alliance. That is why I am a staunch advocate of our membership of NATO. It is not by any means conceivable that Germany would want to or could leave NATO. A return to the old nationalistic ideas of military and economic solo efforts is unthinkable for an exporting country like ours. After all, our country has learned from its deviations, from the hurrah-patriotism with which it went into World War I. And from the disaster in which National Socialism and its megalomania ended. My generation and the following one have learned their lessons. We know how important it is to have the Americans as friends. We just have to be careful that it doesn't make us too lethargic and comfortable.

> *The alliance with the United States, the transatlantic partnership and the affiliation with the West, as surveys in Germany prove, are losing support among Germans. Does that worry you, particularly since you regard our affiliation with NATO to be so important?*

This is indeed a worrying phenomenon. It indicates general insecurity about our position in our bumpy world. It also indicates how difficult it is for politicians to make themselves understood. And it indicates the deficits in our media about which we spoke at another point. That also stems from the fact that in central Europe we cannot possibly imagine that there could be a military conflict in Europe again.

Even now in the Ukraine crisis, I do not get the impression that an awareness of the newly emerged dangers has awakened among the wider population. Who seriously thinks that the tensions with Russia that have ignited because of Ukraine could swell into a hot war? But the danger that it could happen is real.

That is precisely why I added my signature to the appeal about which we spoke at the beginning of this dialogue. We warn against underestimating the conflict. We warn against expecting Putin and thus Russia to accept humiliations that insult the national pride that still exists there. Does the U.S. president have to humiliate the Russians publicly by downgrading them to a regional power? The Russians have a pronounced national pride. Their territory has shrunk because of the new independent states on the Russian periphery. However, they have certainly not become a regional power like Switzerland or Luxembourg.

> *Is that not an invitation to Russia to take back its old spheres of influence in the former Soviet territory, even using military pressure like in Ukraine?*

Both sides, NATO and Russia, must be conscious of the limits of their power, must know where they have to be considerate to the respective other side. That also applies to the Western sanctions and the Russians' retaliatory moves. The EU still has many economic connections to Russia. Both sides must have an interest in not smashing everything that has developed with regard to economic cooperation and mutual trade. I am afraid that a downward trend could commence in Russia that no one could stop any more. The Western sanctions are not only hurting Putin's followers, but also the common people. Let us just remember the devaluation of the Russian currency. That can promote uncontrollable developments.

The Russians have the trauma that their national territory has shrunk drastically since the end of the Soviet Union through the secession of Ukraine, Georgia and the Baltic States. Many consider this to be a humiliation. That cannot be overlooked. I am afraid that because of the Western sanctions the Russian economy will continue shrinking and the population will be affected increasingly hard. Then Putin will find himself in a highly precarious position; he will come under pressure from below. What is the proven method for solving such problems? Quite simply to provoke a huge conflict outside the country to gather the citizens behind him. We are already seeing the preparations for this. I see this as the largest problem, that Putin, if the Russians are increasingly badly off, will build up a conflict like this to distract from the internal problems and to gather the population behind him. I hope I am wrong. We cannot possibly wish for a destabilisation of this type in Russia.

> *Putin has high approval rates in Russia. The capture of Crimea and the successes of the separatists in Ukraine are attributed to him. A new Cold War has already begun.*

A lot of things point that way. There was already a cover story to this effect in the "Spiegel." In the appeal that you mentioned in your first question, the dangers are made clear. Let me quote from it verbatim: "The Ukraine conflict shows: The addiction to power and dominance has not been overcome. In 1990, at the end of the Cold War, we all hoped it would be so. However, the successes of the policy of détente and the peaceful revolutions made us drowsy and careless. In the East and the West to the same extent. Among Americans, Europeans and Russians, the central theme of banishing war permanently from their relationship has been lost. Otherwise, the eastward expansion of the West without simultaneous consolidation of the collaboration with Moscow, that appears threatening to Russia, as well as the annexation of Crimea by Putin in violation of international law, cannot be explained."

In Berlin, the government wants to develop a new concept for our security policy. That is urgently needed. Russia has to be involved in it. There will be no lasting security in Europe without Russia.

> *Do you understand the concerns of the Baltic States and Poland which are emanating from the Russian Ukraine policy and from earlier Russian campaigns in the border region of Georgia?*

Of course. NATO is the most important security factor for Poland and the Baltic countries. And one must certainly acknowledge that NATO has fulfilled its task superbly and was a guarantee of freedom in Europe. However: As much as I am an advocate of NATO, I am equally against our taking on new risks. Admitting Ukraine into NATO, which the government in Kiev and parts of the West want, would end in a catastrophe. That could provoke a world war. A new expansion of the EU towards the East would also bring down this danger upon us. On the other hand, I assume that the Russian president is also aware of the latent dangers and has no interest in provoking a war. Therefore he certainly won't attack Lithuania, Latvia, Estonia. They are members of NATO and the EU. That is a different story from Ukraine or Georgia. The greatest dangers will arise if initially limited conflicts deteriorate into an uncontrollable situation. Who can counteract this eerie scenario apart from Putin?

> *Russia violated international law in annexing Crimea. However, we will make no progress by answering one breach of law with another. If we wish to maintain constitutional principles and international law agreements in international relations, must we not then also demand that Russia observes international law and the right to self-determination?*

Yes, we must. But not unilaterally. We Germans contributed to the collapse of Yugoslavia when we recognised Croatia unilaterally. What did the United States do with Kosovo? It supported the secession from Yugoslavia. The United States cares very little about international law when it enforces its interests, regardless of where in the world that is. What is the United States doing in Guantanamo? Obama took office with the announcement that he would close Guantanamo as early as the middle of his second term of office. But the camp still exists today. Or what is the United States doing with the espionage of its NSA which even wiretaps our Chancellor's telephone. Is that not reminiscent of the McCarthy era, when every citizen was a suspect, so to speak?

> *Putin's politics of defiance has intensified in recent months, and there are statements coming, for example from the chairman of the German-Russian Forum, Matthias Platzeck, former minister-president of the state of Brandenburg, that Russia's annexation of Crimea should now not only be accepted under international law, but legitimised. Do you share this opinion?*

I would not like to comment on that. These are questions of constitutional law to which one cannot give a final answer as a layperson. The German-Russian Forum is a civil society organisation with competent and honourable members. Institutions that unite instead of driving apart are important, particularly in the crisis of German-Russian relations.

Mr Putin recently gave an interview on German television. He argued adeptly. He referred to the Kosovo case. The International Court of Justice in The Hague has declared that the secession of Kosovo from Serbia is legal. The reasoning: If the majority of an ethnic group wants the secession in a democratic process, then it is exercising its right to self-determination. That is exactly what happened in the case of Crimea. The Russians who live there are the majority. They wanted the annexation to Russia. A referendum was held on this which the supporters of the annexation won.

And apart from that, one must also see that it is insulting and demeaning when President Barack Obama characterises Russia as a regional power. The statement is also incorrect. Russia is still a major power in international politics, with a permanent seat and veto power on the United Nations Security Council. After all, the Russians could make fun of the Americans too. Because the Americans need the Russians to transport their astronauts to the International Space Station. If the Russians currently did not have the ability to guarantee supply with their Soyuz rockets, the Americans could neither get to the space station nor back to Earth.

Russia is sending its nuclear bombers out on missions again as far as North America. How should that be interpreted?

That is always a question of perspective. I will not allow myself be manipulated by the suggestion that Putin is the only bad guy. Nonetheless, I see that radical power politics are being practiced demonstratively on the part of the Russians. On the other hand, Putin has been provoked by the West. Former German Chancellor Gerhard Schröder has rightly voiced the criticism that we have squandered too much trust in our relationship with Russia, and that, together with the Russians, we have to get away from confrontation and find a way back to cooperation again, and break out of the spiral of accusations and threats.

The Russians did not contravene international law if protests are now coming that they fly off the Canadian coast with long-range bombers, since this is occurring over international waters. They are doing the same thing that the Americans are doing too. That is basically nobody's business – except, naturally, that the United States and Canada feel threatened, of course. Because after all the Russians could have bombs, or even nuclear bombs, on board. I believe that Putin and the entire Russian government overall are clever enough that they regard the state of a nuclear balance of power to be still in existence today. If they carried out a nuclear attack on New York, the Americans would do the same thing to Moscow. We are experiencing – like we already saw in the conflict with the Soviet Union – strategic sandpit games in which each side gives tit for tat. When Obama says that Russia is only a regional power, then Putin flies his bombers off the coast of America and thereby shows the world: We are not a regional power.

One has to put oneself in the shoes of the man and the state on whose doorstep in Poland or the Czech Republic so-called defensive missiles are being deployed. I would not put up with that either.

Haven't the missiles been deployed for two reasons? Firstly out of fear that Russia could attempt to reclaim former territories of the Soviet Union, for example in the Baltic. Secondly as a protective shield against potential attacks by Iran. Are those not justified protection interests on the part of the West in a time when the threat of war is looming again?

Mr Detjen, one speaks of course of defensive missiles, but those are firing missiles that can also be offensive weapons. I do not want to visualise that there could be a third World War. The internet is changing the world. That is what I am banking on. Because people today have such an excellent opportunity to obtain information to an extent that never existed before. But nevertheless we must recognise the dangers of regional wars in Europe as are being seen in the battles in Ukraine or could be seen formerly in the Balkans. That cannot be called anything else but war.

> *Thus it is all the more important to enforce international law, and first and foremost human rights, on a global scale. Those are positions that differentiate open societies from others.*

There are powers in Russia that want just that.

> *Isn't Russia further away from this than ever before since the end of the Soviet Union? Are we not being taken in by wishful thinking here? Where are the first signs of hope for internal reforms? Maybe in the generation after Putin?*

Not maybe – they are entering another society! I repeat: The internet alone will ensure that.

> *You are very optimistic about that. Even under former KGB head Putin?*

Yes, of course. Putin is like all rulers. He wants to safeguard his power as far as possible. But he is also a pragmatist; he realises where he has to give way, where he has to concede. It is unimaginable to me that Russia will take the path back to the USSR, and thus back to communism or a similar type of dictatorship. The people would no longer put up with that.

> *Up to now, little can be seen of a departure in the direction of a more liberal, pluralist society as long as Putin's opponents are being sent to prison or labour camps for specious reasons.*

This will develop. There is opposition to Putin and his power. At the moment, Putin has solved his domestic problems by stirring up the Ukraine conflict. We have already spoken about the old power model of getting domestic backing from external conflicts. However, Putin's power will not last forever. I think that Russia can find its way to a real democracy. At the moment it is still an authoritarian democracy. Nevertheless, Putin did adhere to the constitution after he had ruled as president for two terms. He left office for one term in accordance with the constitution. After all, he could have just said we'll change the constitution.

> *Is there a note of forced optimism in your voice here? After all, the Würth Group has operations in Russia. What role does the Russian market play for the Group?*

An insignificant one. Only a relatively marginal proportion of our sales comes from there. Our Russian business has room for development, despite the Western sanctions that are hitting Russia's economy hard. Yet we are still operating in the black there. However, our profit in Russia shrank by 50 percent in 2014 compared to 2013. But we have no difficulty importing the goods we need for our business in Russia.

> *There has been a building boom in Russia for years. Surely it must be in your best interests not to get cut off from this?*

In Russia we can do what we need to do for our business. If you are alluding to my political position towards Russia with your question, to the fact that I signed the appeal for a different German policy towards Russia – then you are mistaken if you surmise opportunistic connections. There are none. I am sufficiently independent to be able to openly state my political stance as a concerned citizen. I will not let any side dictate my image of Russia. It is just that I don't see only Putinists in Russia, but also the many people in culture and business who are working towards freedom.

> *Too many of them – think of Mikhail Khodorkovsky – disappear too fast behind bars. And the demonstrators against Putin have yielded to nationalist parades.*

In Russia, people's revolts have a tradition, so to speak, even if they were usually crushed violently. In Ukraine, which was part of Russia under the Tsars – Kiev was the Tsars' coronation city – Viktor Yanukovych was ousted by a revolution. Petro Poroshenko, the current president, came to power through a coup. That is not flawless democracy either.

The history of the 20th century teaches us: If political restrictions, the limitation of freedom becomes too oppressive and the economic situation a disaster, then the people rise up and cause a revolution. That was what happened in Egypt, and that was what happened in Ukraine and in north Africa. Nevertheless, we must never forget that the hopes of the people are seldom fulfilled in such processes.

> *These revolutions often trigger a backlash that generates new oppression, as we are seeing in Egypt.*

That is the other side of the one single coin. We in the West often succumb to wishful thinking. We can see this in the example of Syria. If it is evaluated with a certain amount of objectivity, then I think that President Obama understood this: If Assad falls, Syria will become an Islamist theocracy. That is definitely not in the interest of the United States or of the entire West.

> *There is Islamist terror in Putin's Russia too. Many people were killed in attacks in Moscow and other cities. In the current conflict with Russia, is the common interest of preventing the spread of terrorism by Islamist extremists being shattered?*

I hope that rationality will prevent this. I see IS as a problem that is worrying me a lot more than Russia. These people from the so-called Islamic State have announced that they want to reclaim Spain, particularly the mosque in Córdoba. They refer to the fact that they ruled Spain for 500 years. They say: That is our country! The fact that just in recent months the Catholic Church has made up for what it did not do centuries earlier shows how seriously this threat must be taken: It has had its ownership of the cathedral in Córdoba entered in the land register. That is a very striking and significant signal that IS truly is a danger. When they are finished in Syria and Iraq, then they'll go to southeast Turkey and to Europe. They are so fanaticised that they could advance as far as Vienna in Europe like the Turks did in the 17th century. They could also probably gain access to nuclear weapons easily if they came to power in Pakistan. Pakistan is an unstable country with nuclear weapons. I shudder at the thought that an Islamist theocracy with nuclear arms could become established somewhere.

That should worry us all. The conflict zones on Russia's borders are our neighbourhood. The Mediterranean region is our front yard. If you ask the question of whether our consciousness of the significance of the Mediterranean region and North Africa is adequate for our security in Europe, then my answer is: A more pronounced awareness of latent dangers would be desirable in Europe.

The entire Maghreb and the eastern Mediterranean are a powder keg. Israel is also involved here and implementing a wrong policy. I regret this even more because I have friends in Israel. The fact that Israel is unable to find a way to contribute constructively so that young Palestinians get attractive prospects for the future is having grave consequences – as far as Europe. Israel's settlement policy is also contributing to this. It is taking more and more land away from the Palestinians and thus preventing the creation of a Palestinian state. It is such a deadlocked situation that hate and revenge have flourished so far. I fear that it could end in a huge disaster.

> *The close transatlantic partnership with the United States has always been an essential component of Europe's strength. The Americans have taken over our responsibilities, for example in the Middle East – which is right on our doorstep. Can Europe act without the United States in the conflict zones around the Mediterranean?*

Certainly not from a military aspect. If we are talking about Syria, we have to take the other centres of conflict in the Middle East into consideration as well. The sanctions are already having a considerable effect in Iran. The government will not be able to sit out the high inflation and the other economic setbacks much longer. Iran will have to make concessions in its nuclear programme. Europe is asserting its weight in the negotiations.

When the Iran problem is solved, the United States will be able to exert more influence with regard to Israel. After all, the Americans are treading heavily on the Israelis' toes; they are pushing for a second state, a Palestinian state. If a Palestinian state can be successfully established and stabilised, then the political problems that could make a war worthwhile will disappear. And the Islamic states in North Africa – Egypt and Libya, Algeria, Morocco – they will be preoccupied with their own problems for decades to come.

Let me be blunt about Syria: Do we have to get involved in Syria, apart from giving humanitarian aid? In my opinion, we have had so many wars in Europe for centuries, why should we take on the responsibility of using military intervention to save Syria? If more serious tensions should develop, for example if Syria and the Lebanon were to become aggressive theocracies – then it will be a different matter. Then we would most certainly have to rearm very quickly and boost our defences accordingly.

> *The German army, the "Bundeswehr," is no longer as strong as it once was. It has been deployed in Turkey, in the Kurdish region of Iraq, in the Balkans, in the frozen or already reignited centres of conflict on the fringes of the former Soviet Union – it does not have a combat mission, but it risks being drawn into battles there. Is Germany overreaching itself?*

I am by no means advocating that we define ourselves by our weaknesses. But we cannot believe that it is sufficient to rely solely on the strength of our economy and the attractive force of the euro. The question of military strength will always be relevant. That is why we need a common security policy in NATO. Of course we have to be geared up for the world as it is in reality.

This is the principle that Switzerland also follows, although it is completely surrounded by the EU and does not border any dormant or even hot centre of conflict. Nevertheless, even today, the Swiss still invest in their old fortifications and buy new fighter jets for their air force. They keep their armaments strong. They can afford to do so. But for what purpose and why the Viggen, the Swedish fighter jets? The fighter jets they had previously bought are now old and never fired a single shot at an enemy. The answer to the question about the reason for maintaining one's own military strength is: Armaments are a type of fire brigade for Switzerland. It has to have them for the worst-case scenario.

We always have to answer the question pragmatically: From where is a looming threat emanating, where could the enemy be? Which type of armaments do we need for what? Since the Communists have no longer been in power in Russia, we have been disarming on a large scale in Europe. The defence industry depends on exports to regions outside Europe, because defence expenditure was slashed here in Europe. Nevertheless, we took military action in the conflicts in the Balkans, and the Bundeswehr went to war in Afghanistan.

In central Europe, we are strongly driven by the wish that the peace we have had for a long time in our country is a type of gift from God and that we will not have to do any more than we have done up to now to secure it externally. That makes it more difficult to make the military provisions for the crisis situations that can always occur.

Chapter 3
Appeal for a United States of Europe

Europe needs a fiscal equalisation scheme

The crises are driving us to more unification / However, the old national structures are still having effects underground / Bureaucracy in Brussels is holding Europe together

> *Never before has the European Union been called into question so strongly by anti-European powers than in the second decade of our millennium. At the same time, crises like the one in Greece are weakening the EU. Are you still the passionate European that you have characterised yourself as so many times?*

But of course! The crises are a challenge to the pro-European powers; they have to see them as an incitement to press ahead with unification. European unification is not a project with short-term prospects. It is a historical undertaking which, although it has its roots in European history, has no model that we can just simply copy.

The idea of a peace zone in Europe originated in the aftermath of the major European wars. It became the liberal antithesis to the Communist encroachment into Europe. The idea is more topical today than ever before. The conflicts, of which the war in Ukraine is only one example, can only be resolved in a European peace zone that incorporates Russia. The United States of Europe is also the foundation on which Europe will get a chance to hold its own alongside the superpowers of China and the United States. My hypothesis is: The United States of Europe will emerge from the crisis. However, that will not be easy, but rather laborious.

> *Those are rational arguments that the alienated supporters of nationalist movements increasingly refuse to accept. Can the emotionally driven fears of globalisation, financial manipulation and criminal corporations that are suffused with conspiracy theories still be counteracted with political reason?*

I would not be a liberal if I did not believe in the power of reason. It will not get any easier if uncertainties run rampant, if the trust in the institutions, on whose reliability the stability of open societies is based, ebbs in Western societies.

We should not forget: The Enlightenment emanated from Europe. Even today, we can observe again and again: Where there is no enlightenment, democracy lacks strong roots. For example, in the former Ottoman Empire or in the world of the orthodox churches like in Russia. Incidentally, enlightenment is a perpetual task among ourselves here in Europe too. That irrationality of the anti-Europeans substantiates that.

We should beware of false arrogance or deceptive self-assurance. Nothing happens by itself. Politics must bring Europe forward further. The media cannot always disseminate news about Europe first and foremost as a crisis, but must inform about the positive aspects of unification more than heretofore. We have never had as much common ground in all aspects of life in Europe as we do today. Fifty percent of the entire legal framework of our everyday political, social and economic lives in the EU is based on common European law. That is a strong foundation for the future – and a bulwark against relapses into nationalism.

> *The Front Nationale in France, UKIP in the UK and the AfD in Germany. A dialectic process: The stronger Europe becomes, the more the anti-European powers come out of the shadows. Are there not justified reasons why many doubt that politicians in Germany and in the other countries are capable of warding off the dangers that lie in the temptations of nationalism?*

Fortunately, the European awareness is growing too, despite all backward-oriented national attempts. Surveys in all countries in the EU prove this. Not even the Greeks want to dispense with the EU and the euro. Whenever the threat becomes tangibly perceivable in Europe because of terror, the awareness increases that we will only be able to maintain our accustomed security in our daily lives with a joint defence. In that respect, the dangers coming from outside are bringing Europe together.

Would it have been imaginable even a few years ago that in a crisis like the one over Ukraine, the Europeans would be able to negotiate with Russia without the United States? French President François Hollande and German Chancellor Angela Merkel showed how this can be done. Through negotiations they put a European focus on a crisis where a deployment of U.S. troops would increase the dangers.

At the same time, however, we must recognise that most people below the European level are still rooted and feel at home in their national structures. That is where their emotional bonds lie, their sense of emotional security, the familiar sense of community. That is where the people have their social skin. And most people's are thin. Society is their protective shell. It conveys security. Society creates insecurity when its accustomed structures collapse, when unknown powers – like currently migration – infiltrate its most intimate environment. When Islamist terrorists in our midst prepare attacks or Islamist terrorists from our society go to fight jihad in Syria or Iraq – those are threat scenarios we were not prepared for.

For the first time, many people are currently experiencing globalisation from an aspect they find terrifying – the poor and hungry are pushing into the living spaces of the wealthy and sated. That is reminiscent of the mass migrations in the history we know.

We should not underestimate the national movements that are capitalising on the consequences of globalisation. We have to counteract them more vehemently than heretofore. That is a task for politics – and also for the media. We have to take the fears that are being expressed in these movements seriously. Their rejection of European integration and the euro is embedded in their revolt against the globalisation of all areas of our lives, against so-called financial capitalism, against the expansion of the free-trade zones. Anti-Western resentments are merging here with the groups who reject modernisation.

> *Parties like the AfD in Germany, the nationalists in the Netherlands, the isolationists in the United Kingdom and the French nationalists are propagating in areas where established politics has left room for them. Is European politics only discovering its own shortcomings now?*

I believe there are no single causes to explain this. We should not let ourselves be tempted to make comfortable simplifications. Nor can we succumb to the error of mistaking strong and particularly vociferous minority positions for the majority that still thinks and votes European. In the media, the negative tendencies are being reinforced more than the positive ones, meaning the pro-European majorities, are emphasised. The media reinforce the negative tendencies because they gain them more attention than the benefits that we in Germany in particular get from the EU.

> *In another section of our dialogue, we discuss your much farther-reaching criticism of the media.*

The greatest danger lies in the fact that the anti-European minorities are generating so much insecurity in the societies of the EU countries that Europe's stable core is collapsing. In all the countries where anti-European movements emerge, we observe at the same time a decline in confidence in the parties that have built up Europe over decades. This anti-European reflex has even spread in Switzerland since it has been more closely interconnected with the EU.

> *You believe that a European fiscal equalisation scheme is necessary. That is an unpopular idea in Germany. What leads you to speak out in favour of such a contentious proposition?*

Because I see fiscal equalisation as a foundation that Europe needs for its integration. The crisis that has arisen regarding Greece's membership in the Eurozone and in the EU also teaches us this. We need a mechanism similar to the one among the German federal states. If we do not achieve that, we will endanger Europe's existence. And we need the unification of Europe in order to be able to live in freedom and peace on our Old Continent.

I too want to pay as little as possible. It figures. I do not want to force our money onto the Greeks or anyone else. But I am not only a Hohenlohe man who is very attached to his home *(Heimat)*, a liberal native of Baden-Württemberg, a history-conscious German. Despite all opposition, I am still a passionate European. In light of the power distribution in global politics, Europe only has a chance for retaining its peaceful coexistence in the development of European unification. That is why I am advocating a European solidarity between the wealthy states and those facing bankruptcy.

What use is European fiscal equalisation to the Germans? Why is it in our interest not only to act as guarantor, but where necessary also to pay for Greece, for Spain, for Portugal?

Quite simply: To maintain and reinforce the Eurozone as a unified entity, as the core of the European Union. Monetary union is still young, after all. It is still at the fledgling stage, with many imperfections. We already have almost automatic alignment tendencies within the various countries. The Greeks, the Spanish have to relinquish wages or portions of wages because of their countries' lack of competitiveness. That is a little bit of European alignment of labour costs.

In terms of productivity, incomes in Germany are much lower than in Greece, although the Greeks earn less money in absolute terms than the Germans in comparable professions. The problem is that productivity is far lower in Greece than here in Germany.

Here is an example: If productivity is four times higher here in Germany than in Greece, but wage costs are twice as high as in Greece, then the expenditure per production unit in Germany is only half as high as in Greece. That means: In order to become competitive, the Greeks will have either to reduce their wages further or up their productivity.

That is a protracted and very difficult process. It can take thirty, fifty years until this unified currency area has also been created with regard to labour costs and productivity. And it will take just as long until the divergence in the underlying conditions in other areas is brought to an end, for example in interest rates. During the euro crisis, Greek government bonds were getting interest of three percent, our German bonds were only getting 1.2 percent.

The Greeks say: We are paying for the cheap money that is ultimately benefitting Germany. Thanks to our plight, German banks are getting cheap money and subsequently giving it to us as financial aid – at a disproportionately high interest rate from a Greek perspective.

Germany is profiting from these different structures within the Eurozone because of the fact that the southern European countries are pushing down the euro in international exchange rates. It helps us Germans enormously if the euro does not become too strong. If we were to return to the deutschmark, the valuation of the deutschmark would increase so quickly that our competitiveness would decline. A new deutschmark would probably correspond to a multiple of a euro. Thus our products would be much too expensive around the world.

To that extent, this braking component for the euro-dollar exchange rate or the euro exchange rate against other currencies is very welcome indeed. However, it is almost impossible to make this clear to German citizens. The interdependencies and facts are difficult for most citizens to understand. It is a Herculean task. I can see no one today who can master it.

> *None of the crisis-stricken countries wants to give up the euro and return to their old cheap currency. If the European project is to succeed, politicians with strong leadership will be required. Where are they?*

That is my wish too. Unfortunately, we have no Charles de Gaulle, no Konrad Adenauer, no François Mitterand and no Helmut Kohl any longer. Those were personalities who knew how to convince people – with their passion for Europe. Maybe they had this power of persuasion because they had emerged as Europeans from the wars that had destroyed Europe. I believe that the EU will do well under the new EU Commission President Jean-Claude Juncker. The man is a convinced European. He has extensive administrative experience with all EU institutions and is a canny politician.

> *Instead of a project of passion, Europe has turned into an organisation of calculated political management. It does not carry people along, it does not inspire. Can the United States of Europe emerge like this? When even emotions tend to fuel rejection?*

The EU functions astonishingly effectively, even in times of crisis. That is the decisive factor. European law is effective, the European Parliament emerged stronger from the 2014 elections, holidaymakers are happy about the open borders, the euro is still stronger in an international currency comparison than at its launch, the common market benefits business and consumers who can find Spanish ham, French cheese, Italian wine and Hungarian salami in every supermarket. Those who whinge the most are the people who profit from these European achievements. But those who are not participating would like to. That is why even more states still want to join the EU.

How often has the euro been written off since the crisis broke? The opposite has happened. Many European countries still pin their hopes on the EU for their statutory and economic future. The European Parliament has strengthened democratic structures in the EU. Even if its purchase of government bonds is controversial – the European Central Bank works, it is a strong cornerstone of the common currency and the EU's financing system.

Among the advances are the international banking controls. If you consider that the EU slaps a fine of €800 million on the banks, that is a lot of money. This has closed the door on the speculation with huge money transfers. That did not exist before the introduction of the banking controls. Between 2009 and 2011, many people said everything about the euro was breaking down anyway. There was a flight out of euros. That was a time of European defeatism. What actually happened, in contrast, was a huge advance. The euro crisis has taken a back seat. The EU is showing its teeth.

I believe that no one here in Germany can really imagine what consequences a collapse of the EU would have for our lives – politically, economically, culturally. The EU was and is the deciding factor for peace in Europe. That is why we should be happy that it works so well, even though there are sometimes setbacks and political deadlocks.

> Will the euro ever attain the charisma that the deutschmark once had? The deutschmark was the symbol of Germany's resurgence out of the ruins of World War II. Here in Germany, the euro has not yet achieved a comparable symbolic power for the unification of Europe, although everyone finds it nice when they go on holidays and can pay with the same money everywhere.

Constitutional expert Paul Kirchhof once wrote in a piece for the Frankfurter Allgemeine Zeitung: "Money is minted freedom." That is a really lovely statement. The euro is the expression of freedom in Europe.

For young people, it is such a matter of course to be able to pay with the euro in Lisbon like at home. Having the same money is always an expression of a uniform basis. This is where common thought processes arise.

Remembering the deutschmark is like remembering the GDR. Today, many people in eastern Germany still say: "A lot of things were better in the GDR." But no one wants to go back to the GDR. And it is just the same with the deutschmark. I do not think that there are many among the young people who want the deutschmark back again. The euro is highly attractive internationally. We can see that too in the fact that countries like Latvia and Lithuania have joined the euro. More than 330 million people live in the Eurozone. A further more than 130 million live in countries that have pegged their currencies to the euro. The euro is a success story that cannot be regarded too highly.

My hypothesis is this: At some stage, the UK will not be able to get around joining the euro. But the British, well, they always do it like that. They pick out their advantages everywhere. Look at how they treated the EFTA. But when they realised that the European Union was coming after all, then they jumped up – but only half-heartedly.

The British were always far away from the continent in their "splendid isolation." With its monarchy and the associated social and political structures, the United Kingdom also has a life of its own which is off-putting to many Europeans. But the industrial and business associations know where their business is. Seventy percent of the United Kingdom's exports go to countries in the EU. The British are pragmatic. That could be seen in the referendum on Scotland's secession. The majority was in favour of staying in the United Kingdom. If the British have a referendum on staying in the EU, then I believe it is also quite possible that reason will win over the emotions that are calling for an exit from Europe. If the United Kingdom remains in the EU, then it will probably also join the euro sometime.

Because the economic power in the EU is so strong?

Exactly. Economic power gives strength. Most European citizens understand that they will be crushed between China and the United States if they do not stand together. Every individual little country – Germany and Sweden and Belgium and Finland or whichever – is a dwarf compared to

China and the United States. However, when we see the European Union, then that is more than 500 million citizens. That is more people than in the United States and more than a third more than in China. That is substantial. Then you can have a say in world politics. Through the euro, our situation in the world got a fundamental boost.

And we must not forget this: European awareness does not just develop through the alignment of the legal systems, through the common currency area, through European involvement in Africa or Latin America or through joint anti-terror operations by the armed forces. European awareness grows from below, where citizens from the states of the EU meet on the lowest organisational levels of politics, meaning the local level.

One example of this is the many town twinnings. As the largest central European country, we in Germany in particular need close human relationships with our most important neighbours. That is why it is so positive that almost half of all municipal partnerships have been forged with cities and municipalities in France and Poland. If we want to bring Europe forward, the fostering of acquaintanceship, of integration, of amalgamation at the level of people's local and regional living spaces is a very important component. And we must not forget: Tourism promotes integration too.

You have created a global company. How do you see the development of the euro against the dollar and the Asian currencies?

The euro will definitely stay strong, even if it is subject to fluctuations against the dollar and the Swiss franc. The yuan will become one of the three reserve currencies alongside the dollar and the euro. The euro is not positioned strongly enough everywhere yet. When I am travelling in South America, I see that you still have the disadvantage that the dollar is more in demand in everyday life there.

There is strong competition between the United States and Europe for dominance on the financial markets.

It probably would have been alright with the Americans if the euro had failed. As to the fact that a euro is worth more than a U.S. dollar, that was different at the beginning, after all. That goes against the grain for Americans. Of course, there are always forecasts that say: In a few years, the euro will be worth less than the dollar. That may be the case temporarily. If the banks cannot manipulate any exchange rates any more, like they did in the past, thanks to the stricter controls on the part of the EU, then the exchange rates will develop more than heretofore alongside real purchasing power and the incredibly large economic performance in the Eurozone. Fluctuations will still remain.

> *Scepticism has grown in the United States towards the German position on currency and fiscal policy. Nobel prizewinner Paul Krugman is the protagonist in the New York Times of the demand: "Germany must abandon its austerity policy and make more debts." Tensions are erupting here in transatlantic relationships that were never seen before. Are we causing the United States economic problems because we are so strong?*

The Americans are used to having the import surplus. Evidently, $ 300 billion are insignificant there. That is definitely a bubble that will burst sometime. At the latest when the Chinese no longer buy any U.S. bonds, any Treasuries. Then things will get tight for the United States. The Americans currently have more interests in the Pacific region than in Europe. They want to protect Japan, they do not want to lose Taiwan and have China as their greatest adversary.

In addition to the differences in fiscal policy, the relationship to Europe is strained because of the NSA affair and the refusal to sign an anti-spying agreement. The Americans say, we are friends, but we don't trust you. Everyone entering the United States can experience this when they have to wait for two hours at passport control after an eight- or ten-hour flight.

> *Europe is much more than euro, army, economic power. The United States emerged from the spirit of Europe. Your personal commitment to art and the Würth Group's cultural activities transcend the old national boundaries. Do you see your involvement in culture as a contribution to the European project?*

Europe has always been an intellectual power that emanated worldwide. The Würth Group's cultural commitment is based on this awareness, even if we can only offer a drop in the ocean with our modest resources. We use them to enable art and history to be experienced in their European dimensions. And we are participating in the continuation of the construction of European history. Here, in its culture, is Europe's reality. That is most effective in top-level culture, and thus among the elite. That is why we need elites in science and culture, in order that Europe can progress further.

If we are realistic, we have to admit: The elite are those who ultimately decide the fundamental things. In the United States ten percent leads the country, takes the country forward, turns the country into a world power. Europe has a lot to catch up on there. That is why we also promote schools, universities and scientific projects.

> Your museums, your art collection, your forums communicate a message to the outside. Does that also apply to the communication with the employees in your company?

Yes of course! That is a contribution to the European consciousness. Our companies are profoundly European. Through fifteen art rooms, art museums, art institutes in ten European countries – including Germany – employees in their work environment and visitors to our programmes experience that culture cannot be constrained into narrow geographic or national spaces.

Almost 45,000 of our 66,000 employees work in the EU. We operate in all European countries; to us, no political borders really exist in the EU any more. Not even to Switzerland. If one looks at it correctly, Switzerland is to a large extent indirectly integrated into the EU economically.

We have begun closing down our warehouse in Belgium and we are supplying customers from Germany. Within the company, Belgium is like a European federal state. That is the progress in the EU, that we also are becoming integrated within the company, above and beyond national borders. That is what the European Commission wants. They want to close all the loopholes that enable one of the states to have special rights or that prevent freedom of movement. I find that wonderful: The Commission wants to enforce that Europe becomes like one country in every respect.

How do exchanges work in the company? How important are language barriers? The Swiss, the natives of Chur, can speak German like the employees in Waldenburg or Künzelsau. But Spanish, French, Chinese, Italians have to overcome language barriers.

That is no problem at all. Today, English is the lingua franca in the international network. Young people today experience this as a matter of course, after all: The main language of the EU is English and at the same time the local languages are still spoken. The various languages will increasingly take a back seat in business life. In our company, we already hold thirty percent of all our conferences in English. On Monday and Tuesday I gave my lecture in Bad Mergentheim, for the University of Louisville, in English. We have departments in the company that operate only in English. The computer scientists' conversational language is English.

We have Spanish employees who grew up here as children and then returned to Spain, and today speak perfect German like we do with no accent whatever. In addition, they speak perfect Spanish. And if they then, for example, become salespeople, then English is added. Language barriers are not a problem for European integration.

World War I began a hundred years ago with the murder in Sarajevo. The old Europe went down with it. Today, most people in Europe probably believe that an event like the murder in Sarajevo could no longer trigger a war. Is this a misapprehension? Former Chancellor Kohl said: "Europe is a question of war and peace." Chancellor Merkel expressed a similar opinion. Could Europe become a war zone once again because of internal conflicts?

Certainly not in the short term. But if we are not careful, a relapse can occur in the long term. The Franco-German relationship is still on shaky foundations. We swear friendship and good cooperation. We are building Europe together, the Germans and the French. But underneath, the vestiges of old prejudices and rivalries still lie dormant.

Particularly in Franco-German relations, we have to be incredibly mindful that we foster this relationship and that we deal with each other exceptionally delicately. Europe will still be a task for future generations too. We only have to experience a few more elections like there was in Austria, with these brownshirt voters who were gathered around a politician named Haider. It has already been almost forgotten that there was an EU boycott of Austria. And if the nationalists from the Front National in France were to make further progress... That could indeed lead to a critical conflict situation.

> *So the consolidation of Franco-German relations is still a basic prerequisite for the further development of Europe?*

Precisely. I have been to an economic forum of German and French top managers and entrepreneurs several times, the Rendez-vous d'Evian. I once had a bad experience there during the presentation of a state secretary from the German Finance Ministry. In the presence of the then French President François Mitterrand, the state secretary behaved with an unbearable arrogance. The way he emphasised Germany's power in the EU – that was poison for Franco-German relations.

> *You are embedded in the tradition of southern German liberalism and federalism. Do you have a liberal guiding principle for Europe's future? Does the Brussels centralism still allow those things that are the central points of liberal postulates: autonomy and subsidiarity? Or is Brussels shaping Europe with statism and centralism according to the French model?*

The philosophy of liberalism is certainly effective. Even in the United Kingdom. It is interesting that a three-party system has emerged in the United Kingdom, although there were only two parties there for centuries. Now the Liberals have managed to get into Parliament with direct mandates. So – if liberalism shows itself clearly, it will have an infectious future in Europe.

> *Liberalism develops from civic presence, from civic life, civic thought and civic independence. Is there such a thing as a European citizen? Or is that not necessary at all, because it is sufficient to be a native of Hohenlohe with a European outlook? You are a native of Hohenlohe and admit to it, and at the same time you are a European and a cosmopolitan.*

There are millions of others like this too. It is a huge mixture of origin, experience, formation by the environment and the vision that one has for the future. If you take all these components together, those would be the ideal conditions in a state, if there really was a liberal ethos there, if all citizens had a liberal attitude, were tolerant, acted autonomously, repressed subsidiarity as much as possible and simply gave absolute top priority to civil rights, civil liberties. Europe in its diversity is a model for civil liberties – but only if we protect them. That is why the methods of the secret services in the United States are unacceptable to us. NSA accomplices and consorts are lethal for liberalism.

> *But so is that which is commonly described as Brussels centralism, surely?*

Up to a certain degree, we need centralism. Liberalism can also be partially centralistic. Liberalism cannot do without state power. An administration system consists of reciprocating movements. Liberalism needs law and order too.

In the situation we are in at the moment, we need the Brussels centralism. There is no other way, otherwise every country would do what it liked again. And the Germans would not implement the Brussels provisions into national law at all, the Italians and the French even less so, and then Europe would fall apart again. So: Centralism benefits Europe – at its current stage of development. It cannot be dispensed with until there are enough common structures in place, until the borders have really been razed and no one considers introducing border controls again anymore; then, I think, the regions can be strengthened again and can become more federalist – but at the moment we need this heavy hand that will ultimately bring the project to its goal.

> *Would Europe drift apart if there was not such a strong bureaucratic power exerting influence in Brussels?*

At the very least, the continuation of the unification process would be endangered. The self-serving interests are still too big, especially those of the national politicians who see their re-election at risk. Brussels has to be strong to bring Europe forward. And I believe that this is proven by the national politicians: They shift as many weak people as possible from their parties to Brussels. Then the national politicians have more power over the players in Brussels than if the strongest had been delegated to the European positions. It can only be hoped that the European Parliament makes even more of a mark than it has done up to now. Thankfully, that has already begun. The Parliamentarians will no longer put up with everything and are defiant.

The European Parliament gained a respectable and gratifying self-assurance from the 2014 European elections. It asserted that it can elect the Commission President and that all Commissioners require its approval. The Parliament and the Eurogroup of the EU collaborated to build bridges for the Greeks – whether that can prevent a "Grexit" is questionable. Even in this crisis, the EU proved itself. I hope that this can be sustained. After all, we are speaking in a time in which the problems with Greece have not yet been solved, war is raging in Ukraine and Russian policy is controversial.

Chapter 4:
The free entrepreneur and politics

In the liberalist tradition

Too much state destroys the citizen's individual responsibility / The FDP's failure / A free society needs to be fostered by the elite

> *You have dealt with principles of corporate management and structures in your lectures and in many speeches. You demand leadership skills and goal orientation. Can that which brings companies success be applied to the state, to state actions?*

I am happy that I am not a politician. As an entrepreneur, you have different scope for action. You have more power and more freedom. To that extent, principles of corporate management only have limited applicability to state institutions and social processes.

In politics, other rules apply than in business. We recently experienced a prominent example of this in how one of our most successful German politicians failed two years after he switched to business. I am speaking about the former minister-president of Hesse, Roland Koch. A good politician is not necessarily a good entrepreneur. After all, if they dare to make the switch, politicians are usually used as liaison people in their old network of connections. Mercedes got Mr Eckart von Klaeden, the former state secretary at the Federal Chancellery to do this. At German rail company Deutsche Bahn, the former Bavarian economics minister joined the management board. He has now retired. But Deutsche Bahn is immediately getting itself another politician – the former head of the Federal Chancellery. In the end of the day, this is how politicians become lobbyists and get better pay.

All experience shows: If politicians decide what companies should and should not do, it usually goes wrong. Look at the scandals at the Landesbanks, for example in Bavaria, where the hole that came about through the politically engineered deal with Hypo Alpe Adria Bank had to be plugged with billions in taxpayers' money. Look at the disasters of the major Berlin airport and the Nürburgring. That does not just affect the individual federal state, but all taxpayers. Because incinerating such huge tax revenues ultimately affects everyone.

If an entrepreneur permits himself such errors of management, then he goes bankrupt, and deservedly so. But what happens to the politicians who are sitting on the supervisory bodies of such projects? What happens to the managers who were heaved out of politics into management positions at the state-controlled companies and institutions – who themselves were often previously active politicians?

Have we too much state economy here in Germany?

We have too much state. That is the result of the decline in liberal principles in our politics. It also stems from the fact that here in Germany more and more people are happy to give up their individual responsibility to the state. And the parties are just as happy to jump on it because it gives them the opportunity to expand their influence.

Liberalism requires that everyone is responsible for his actions. In the areas of the economy which are shaped by state and party-political factors, the responsibility has become collectivised beyond recognition, meaning: A system has emerged in which irresponsible actions can almost no longer be identified in the maze of party-political and state interconnections. As a result, the perpetrators can also hardly be held liable any more. And then even enquiry committees are no use any more.

Companies have a hierarchical structure. Companies' success is achieved hierarchically. This is where lines of responsibility emerge too. Wherever the state is active entrepreneurially, this does not appear to function. Why does society need hierarchies?

That is a difficult issue. There is not just black and white in the world, even if many political saviours would like to convince us of this. Don't all important institutions in our society have a hierarchical structure? The higher court stands over the district court, the Federal Administrative Court decides over the administrative courts of the federal states. Our federal state structure is hierarchical. So: Even in a democratic society, hierarchies are necessary so that everything doesn't get jumbled up. Hierarchies are not undemocratic – at least not with our Basic Laws for the Federal Republic (the German constitution) and the states, in our free constitutional state.

> In our society, both the trade unions as well as weighty voices in the Protestant Church and the majority of the parties are increasingly demanding so-called democratisation. That includes the call for the introduction of democratic structures into companies. That must go completely against the grain for you. In most of your companies, there are not even any works councils.

The system that we have here in Germany today works a bit clumsily, but nonetheless quite well. But that is not the last word on the subject either. Even the workers at VW in the United States proved this when they were asked whether they wanted a works council along German lines. The workers declined. I am always in favour of relativizing things, observing, weighing up, looking at the advantages and disadvantages.

As a liberal, I bank on reason. It dictates that everyone in his own position bears responsibility for the whole. That applies to company management; that applies to the trade unions. If everyone adheres to that, even works councils are useful, of course.

> Nevertheless, the dispute between entrepreneurs and trade unions is a question of power politics. Time and again the social power of trade unions, of business associations and of companies plays an important role in politics. The classic liberalism that counteracts it with civil freedom and individual responsibility appears to be an obsolete model in these circumstances.

If you reduce this topic down to a power play, I do not consent to that at all. Why? That has something to do with my liberal mindset. Liberalism is based on people's ability to think and act reasonably. If we treat each other reasonably we don't have to play any power games. Because I am not naïve I know that life does not always work out like that. However, I want to adhere to this postulate as the fundamental position for social actions. The Works Constitution Act also assumes this capability to act reasonably.

It requires that both partners cooperate in the interest of the employees and the company. Essentially, everyone is in the same boat. If the company is no longer functioning economically, it will go bankrupt. That is why the story with the Lufthansa pilots in 2014 is a prime example of how absurdly the pilots' trade union acted in this case. The pilots, who are being paid annual salaries of between €170,000 and €200,000, should have acted more reasonably. They know the competition in global air transport and the government subsidies that the airlines of the Gulf States, which are at the same time pressuring Lufthansa, are getting. Turkish Airlines is also attracting increasingly more traffic with the development of the hub in Istanbul. If Lufthansa does not watch out, it will be out of the picture in a few years. Then it will become a problem case like that of Alitalia. Then the pilots' high salaries will be no use to them anymore. That is a model for unreasonable behaviour; it can take a company to the brink of disaster.

> *Liberalism is founded, among other things, on the teachings of Adam Smith, which state that in a free society an invisible hand provides the equalisation between self-interest and the public good. In this sense, self-interest requires the consideration of other market participants' interests.*

But that is easy to understand. Anyone who is only egoistic harms themselves. Self-interest has its limits at the juncture where you harm other people in society together with whom you want to live, work, do business and act as a community.

> *As an entrepreneur you are banking on the fact that your employees trust you. That does not work unilaterally. You also have to put your trust in your employees. This runs counter to the social phenomenon that people here in Germany generally trust the state more than private companies and thus more than business overall. Germans trust the state, not you and your entrepreneur colleagues. What did you do wrong?*

But that is so obvious, Mr Detjen! That stems from the fact that the state has developed into a national insurance institution. To put it pointedly and succinctly: Today no one needs personal responsibility any more. Although every newborn child is immediately encumbered with €50,000 in debt, at the same time it also gets a promise of life-long state welfare.

As to the fact that the state in the final analysis always encumbers the citizens with its debts, who actually notices that? My generation and that of our parents experienced three currency changeovers – the end of the gold mark of the German Empire, then the abolition of the reichsmark by the deutschmark and then the replacement of the deutschmark with the euro. The first two were actually national bankruptcies. In government currency manipulations such as these, it is always the little people who are the biggest losers. The state restructures at their expense.

The third currency conversion of these two generations is an exception, because the abolition of the deutschmark was not the result of public over-indebtedness, rather, the political intention was to give the unification of Europe a monetary foundation for its future. Now we and the next generation have to ensure that this great undertaking does not go down the tubes.

The average citizen does not perceive the debts with which the state encumbers its citizens as a personal burden. After all, as a citizen he is provided for, from children's allowance to funeral allowance. The commandment of brotherly love and helping the weak and the poor has degenerated here in Germany into the state promise of maintenance in all areas of life. The person receiving maintenance in this way no longer has the obligation to take personal responsibility. The state promises him that he will not starve, will not freeze, and will get his clothing and his warm apartment. So why should someone who is seduced in such a way vote for the liberals? They say: Kindly assume responsibility for yourselves and fend for yourselves.

That was what the FDP[1] used to say. That is a position that scarcely any politician adopts now. The FDP has disappeared from the political market. Initiatives for individual responsibility find no favour with the sluggish masses.

Chancellor Schröder also felt this very acutely when he pressed ahead with his Agenda 2010. That was a programme with market-based principles. The aim was to prune back the fully comprehensive state. Schröder got no thanks for this, not from the electorate, not from his own party. They left him out in the cold, as they had demonstrated with their Federal Chancellor Helmut Schmidt when the NATO arms escalation with Pershing rockets was at issue in 1982.

> *Historically, the fundamental idea of liberalism developed against the state from England. Is that a tradition of freedom that we lack here in Germany?*

Undoubtedly – here in Germany, after all, one always has the impression that the authorities grant freedom. Of course, you can see where that is leading. In our society, the majority of citizens like the welfare state. They feel good in their mediocrity. That is where the demise of liberalism comes from. And because the FDP did not know how to develop a brand culture. The FDP leadership thought it had to imitate the two mainstream parties to keep votes. Mr Westerwelle and his people thought they had to be electable in all policy fields like the other parties. The FDP made the huge mistake of setting up a general store; they suddenly wanted to be a mainstream party and do everything like the others from social policy through justice and the economy. That was just predestined go wrong! It is totally logical.

I was active a few times for the FDP, once even as a speaker at an election event in Mecklenburg-Western Pomerania. On that occasion, I said, among other things, that the FDP was just simply the party of the higher income-earners. Afterwards, they absolutely devoured me. The FDP people said one just could not say that. This lack of courage to position itself clearly in society was the FDP's downfall. Liberalism lost its home in German politics.

During the elections, the FDP should have said out straight and uncompromisingly: "We represent the interests of the citizens in the Federal Republic who earn higher incomes." Then the FDP would definitely have always got its ten or eleven percent. But what happened instead? Small and medium-sized business, the tradespeople, the high-income white-collar workers no longer felt represented by the FDP. They became party-politically homeless. They did now not know where they should direct themselves politically. In the end, this FDP electorate had no choice but to vote for the Green party or if necessary the CDU. There is no professional representation, no representation of interests in the political arena for small and medium-sized business.

> *So that would then be a great opportunity for a reinvigorated FDP if they set themselves up again as the party of freedom, of personal responsibility…*

And of the higher-income earners!

That does not have to be at the top of the list…

No, Mr Detjen, I think that is absolutely wrong! The first thing they would have to write on their programmes and placards is: "We are the party of the higher-income earners." Why should they hide that – for heaven's sake? That's what they have to say first! End of story! Then the higher-income earners will also be willing to give their vote to the FDP.

Incidentally, the FDP also dropped out of the Bundestag because CDU Chairwoman Merkel had ridden roughshod mercilessly over the FDP when she became Chancellor. Ms Merkel tamed the FDP cruelly. They just could not do anything at all in this CDU-FDP coalition, they were strangled by the CDU.

But the FDP put up with it! Does not politics dictate: Whoever does not stand their ground...

Yes, of course. In the last legislative period, nothing in the FDP manifesto was implemented. They simply ignored the FDP. With party leaders like Guido Westerwelle and whatever they were all called, that is no wonder either. That would not have happened under party leader Hans-Dietrich Genscher. It was a bizarre situation. Party leaders Westerwelle and Rösler were not persuasive personalities. After all, Mr Steinmeier is of a totally different calibre in his role as foreign minister than Mr Westerwelle was. If Walter Steinmeier had been FDP chairman, things would have gone differently for the FDP.

Have not all the so-called mainstream parties, meaning the SPD, the CDU and the CSU, adopted basic tenets of liberalism themselves and partially implemented them in their party programmes? The liberal idea was no longer a unique selling point of the FDP. Liberal positions were heavily absorbed by others in the model of an open society.

But where are these others liberal? I do not see anything liberal; they have become the designers of the national insurance institution!

In the liberalist tradition

> *In social policy – yes. But in other areas of politics, the CDU and CSU, and also the SPD, have migrated from their ideological milieus. For example in education policy, in legal policy, in their attitudes to the arts and with regard to the influences of the churches. Today, figures like Thomas Dehler[2] or also Hildegard Hamm-Brücher[3] lack the resistance they fought against in their time. They were able to use that to hone their liberal profile. The times of a Mr Hundhammer, who as minister for education fought against the coeducation of boys and girls on the Salvatorplatz square in Munich, who put Bertolt Brecht on the index in the schools – that is absolutely unimaginable today. The other parties have dispossessed the FDP of part of their basic principles!*

But that is just talk. I repeat: In their actions, none of this is liberalism! If the FDP really had a liberal philosophy, it would fight against this stupidity of pensions at 63. Just so that you understand me correctly: I am neither against the pensions nor against the compulsory long-term care insurance. I am against the dissolution of the connection to individual responsibility. The principle of subsidiarity has long since been given up – meaning the idea that the state will jump in wherever personal provisions break down through no fault of one's own, where welfare and humanitarianism demand state aid. That is something completely different to the currently prevailing mentality of state-guaranteed all-round maintenance. The state regulates everything, from the cradle to the grave. Thus the achievements of the preceding generations are being punished with contempt and disregard. The generation of our parents and grandparents, when not one person received children's allowance and housing allowance and heating allowance and clothing allowance, brought up their children and let them learn. They saved and made sacrifices for the future of the next generation. Today, the parties are providing for their voters at the cost of the state on the back of future generations.

> *You are describing the perversion of the social market economy. I have always understood that you were an advocate of the social market economy as championed by Ludwig Erhard and his associate Alfred Müller-Armack, including the social obligation of ownership…*

We do not live in a social market economy. We live in a socialist market economy. That is the difference. The Würth Group and my family comply with the social obligation of ownership in many diverse ways.

We both experienced the start of the social market economy. Was it not headway at that time, in order to lay the foundations for a more stable, broadly-based, liberal society? Wasn't the social market economy, in its core ideas of subsidiarity and individual responsibility, the prerequisite for the emergence of a liberal society in Germany? Did the success of the social market economy undermine the FDP?

Not the success, but the perversion – or even more plainly: the abolition. The FDP did not oppose this decisively. That is its problem. That cost the FDP its votes.

In addition, the new generation of politicians is shrivelling. Personalities who once characterised liberalism, from Theodor Heuss to Otto Graf Lambsdorff, are no longer around. The FDP did not only fail in the last election because it allowed itself to be outplayed by German Chancellor and CDU Chairwoman Merkel. It lacked the personalities who attract voters and convince them of the necessity, of the benefits of a liberal policy for society.

Which personalities impressed you politically and shaped your attitudes?

I really liked the first German President Theodor Heuss. I always saw Heuss as a role model. Not just with his political views, but also as a human being. He was easy-going, had a healthy sense of humour and self-mockery. He did not take himself too seriously, at least ostensibly. I did not see this role model as a template for imitation. But this pleasant type of attitude to life and way of behaving just exudes liberalism. That also corresponds to my way of life. I got through life well on it.

Do you have other role models?

My father and my grandfather were definitely role models for me. Particularly my grandfather. He was a real "Do what is right and don't shy away from anyone" person. He still had his Kaiser Wilhelm beard. He was a treasurer at the Württemberg Landessparkasse savings bank in Ilsfeld. He entered every mark that the customers paid in into the savings books in his perfect handwriting. The man was impressive. I spent a lot of my holidays at his house. I was out in the field with my grandfather a lot, we fetched grass there, fodder for the cows.

My father also influenced me. He was relatively strict. Sometimes we got a clip around the ear from him if things did not go the way he had imagined they would.

Such influences within the family are different to that which one detects as exemplary in other personalities. Nelson Mandela impressed me tremendously – his courage, his resilience, his desire for freedom, his firm belief in the feasibility of creating a new world. The world needs figureheads like that, so that the knowledge is retained that freedom sometimes has to be won with sacrifices.

It also needs people like Robert Bosch as figureheads. He was a role model for me as an entrepreneur. He came from a farming family, one of twelve children. Became a Social Democrat and then a Liberal. He is an example of how an entrepreneur can influence a company beyond his own lifetime with his personality and his ideas.

Children need role models. That begins with the children's books. After all, children have the natural impulse to learn from others. I get the impression that this is no longer adequately encouraged here in Germany. Or at least the wrong role models are created too often, for example in the media. Inventors, engineers, discoverers, humanities scholars – where do children get to know them as role models now? Not in the schools, I fear, not in the churches either. For many young people, in terms of being a role model, the family is still a haven of yearning. In practice, fewer and fewer children achieve it. If fifty percent of children in many places grow up with single parents, that is not just a social problem, but a source of deficits that will have bad effects in future generations.

Thus increasingly more of the conditions are disappearing under which liberalism can sustain itself in society, not to mention develop. I am quite old-fashioned in that respect. I wish that family structures would become intact again. Children should experience the family as long as possible as the fundamental structure of our social coexistence. That is why I also support the policy of Bavarian Minister-President Horst Seehofer, who awards a bonus to mothers who care for their children themselves. The experiences of a coexistence that spans generations can be best made in families. Mutual responsibility: Where can children learn that better than in families?

What do you do for this as an entrepreneur?

Yes, all entrepreneurs and companies are called upon here. They have to enable young families to practice their professional work and family life at the same time. In the Würth Group, we have already done a lot for this. I know that it is still not enough. Our next steps will be childcare facilities in the companies. We are currently in the throes of putting a model for this into practice.

If there is a lack of personalities to make the political positions visible in daily life, then the parties lose their appeal.

To become effective, ideas need people to give them an identity. We learn this from history. Incidentally, not just regarding politics. It also applies in companies. There is an idea behind every company. The entrepreneur is the personification of that idea. At least, that is how it should be, I believe.

It applies to you personally.

If you see it like that. I don't mind.

Back to the FDP. Where are the personalities which can give liberalism its faces?

I believe we are going round in circles on this point. If a party's politics are not right, then the young politicians do not feel attracted to join it. I bet that if the FDP were to have as its motto: "We are the party of the higher-income earners," then the FDP would gain the manpower accordingly. Then it would become visible again how important the fundamental ideas of liberalism are for European economic and fiscal policy and thus for the continued success of the German economy. Political liberalism that stands for freedom, for individual personal and internationally recognised human rights, must characterise our international relations, and is part of the further development of education policy and of our understanding of cultural policy. It is about more than social policy here. If the FDP gives itself a brand essence again, then it will also attract those people again who represent its political weight. And then it will also get into the Bundestag again, I am pretty sure of this.

> *The United States has the elite universities like Stanford, Princeton or Harvard that draw talents from around the world. You, Mr Würth, as an entrepreneur foster research projects yourself, you worked in Karlsruhe as a professor, you expedited the establishment of universities in the north of Baden-Württemberg. Has the former model academic country of the Humboldt brothers been left behind internationally?*

Yes, the attractiveness has turned. That stems from the fact that the United States fosters the elite unconditionally and consistently. I will elucidate the difference using an example: The illiteracy rate in the United States is twice as high as in Germany. And nevertheless the Americans receive most of the Nobel Prizes.

> *Is liberalism dying here in Germany because there is a lack of an elite and of an appreciation of elitist successes?*

The doers who realise an idea in society have become rare in politics. It requires political courage to stand up in public against the march into uniformity, against the trend in the entire country to move with the crowd, not to stand out, either at the top or at the bottom. That reaches as far as the education system.

Liberalism does not prevail of its own accord; it requires social structures, people who can look after themselves, and opportunities for free information. Unfortunately, in too many countries, too many of the conditions in which liberalism could flourish are still lacking. There is a lack of civil awareness, of experience with the freedom of the individual, of economic substance, of historical knowledge, of education overall – and particularly of legal security. However, the impetus towards freedom is accelerating everywhere in the world. The internet is promoting this, for example in Russia and in China.

Does a liberal society need the fostering of the elite for its self-preservation?

That is the basic requirement. Sometimes I get the impression that politicians think that if they lower the requirements for education and achievement in schools and universities, they will banish the complexity out of modern life. The opposite is the case. Coexistence in open societies requires more capabilities and skills from people than in the old days when the authorities called the tune. That was rather comfortable. Back then, the borders still applied between the ruled and the rulers. Liberalism removed them and created the open society.

As a result, the role of the elite should become less important. If everyone accepts their responsibility for themselves as individuals and for the states as citizens – is that not a liberal model?

Every society needs models. But it also needs structures and leadership. Who will lay the foundations for this, if not the elite? If a nation does not foster the elite wholesale, it will wallow in the mire of mediocrity and will be unable to permanently hold or achieve any top positions in the globalised business world. In some areas, Singapore is far more advanced today in developing the elite than we or the Chinese are. They are relentless in their efforts. I do not want to idealise this. But the example makes the contrast with the development here in Germany all the more evident.

And we should not understand the term elite in the academic sense alone. It also includes purely technical professions, the engineers, the electronic engineers. And the tradespeople! We tend to think of them far too little when we talk of the elite. Today, the technical craft trades require skills and knowledge that many academically nurtured subjects do not come near.

Our problem is that politics elevates mediocrity virtually to the level of normality in order not to hurt anyone. Luckily, we are still ranked second in global exports. By head of population, we are still ahead of the Chinese with our exports. We still have a top ranking in business and in many areas of technology.

One strength of our business sector is the perpetual learning on the job, learning by doing. However, we are very unlikely to be able to maintain our position unless we achieve a situation where the elite are fostered much more than up to now. If that does not occur, then we will disappear from the world market. The establishment and financial support of elite universities out of the federal government budget shows that the federal government sees that. Fortunately, politicians have realised that priorities have to be set here.

Universities play an important role. Talents must be discovered. The universities owe this service to society. A good teacher at a university or a university of applied sciences recognises which of his students possess particular skills, and he promotes the talented people. That is why our highly state-ruled university system also has the capability to discover and advance the elite.

It is fortunate that even at the federal state level, certain rudimentary changes have been made in the state institutions. I am thinking, for example, about schoolteachers in Baden-Württemberg. Now the Peter principle, that dictates that the person with the longest term of service is promoted, no longer applies there. More attention is paid to achievement and success than used to be.

> *What role can companies play in educating the elite? Do companies find it easier to educate the elite than the state system? Simply because they have a hierarchical structure and work on a hierarchical basis?*

But our outstanding achievements in the export industry are the result of the elite! Successes of the elite of engineers, inventors, innovative entrepreneurs, skilled workers with their precision and reliability, mechanical engineers with their wealth of ideas. They advance our business sector, they do not wait for redistribution and subsidy. Those are elitist systems that are based on high performance, on diligence and a sense of responsibility and ambition. Education within companies is somehow always oriented to the goal: We want to be and remain the best in our market with our expertise and our products.

For the past few years, a congress of world market leaders has taken place every year in Schwäbisch Hall. It started with the mechanical engineers in the region – now more and more participants are coming from all over Germany. This is an elite showing its best side. It is not resting on its laurels because it is a world market leader. It exchanges ideas about how this position can be defended time and again through constant innovation.

However: Companies cannot become politically effective as factors of liberalism like parties or state institutions. In principle it is actually good that our system of government allocates the leading role to parties in the formation of a political will and the implementation of political ideas. That is the basis of parliamentary democracy. Thus I regret all the more that the FDP did not fulfil this task, that it missed this opportunity.

Yet companies and entrepreneurs, with their individual responsibility, are and will remain an important expression of liberality in the day-to-day life of our society. Beset, however, by the expansion of state restriction and regulation.

> *We have a strong tradition of authoritarian thinking. That also has something to do with our church history. Authorities and church have always had a close association. This is where the authoritarian structures and the image of the good ruler who looks after his own developed. Is this also where our notion of the caring state originated?*

Yes, I agree with you on that. That also has to do with the piety that is particularly pronounced here in Württemberg. The people of Baden were way ahead of us in terms of emancipation from the state, became revolutionaries – and ultimately liberals too. The University of Freiburg has played a key role in this up to our own time.

The structure shaped by the authorities in the Protestant Church is not as pronounced today as it used to be. After all, today's ministers are members of the German student generation of 1968. Because of this socialisation, they tend to be against the authorities in their attitudes.

> *Even the former '68 generation values the system of church tax. But that promotes their attachment to the state.*

That is quite true. But whether we take the long way round or the direct route, it always leads to the same point: The state in Germany has simply developed into a general insurance for life.

The growing faith in the nanny state in Europe is in opposition to another tradition in the United States. The liberal principle of the limitation of the state and the precedence of individual responsibility is alive and kicking right into the Democratic Party in the United States. Does it make Mr Würth the Liberal happy to see this?

Even in the United States, party considerations ultimately apply. We can see that from the obstacles that are constantly being placed in President Obama's way by the Republicans and even by members of his own party. In the United States, liberalism as we understand it today is limited to the intellectual oases on the East Coast and to biotopes on the West Coast. According to my observations, society in the United States is deeply divided, both socially and in its significant political structures. In its foreign policy with a growing tendency to turn its back on Europe! Another generation is proliferating here. This one no longer has any historical roots in common with Europe like the previous one did, and from which NATO was established as a Western alliance with Europe.

In our generation, we have experienced how society moved toward the left, drawn by an ideologically inspired power. Those were the years of the '68 generation and the time that followed them. At that time, the maelstrom in society did not emerge from the promise of state-guaranteed all-round maintenance. The energy stemmed from the belief in the ability to conquer capitalism by changing social structures. In retrospect it appears that the expectations back then were directed towards having less state, not more state. How did you experience that?

I did not really bother about it much. I had to work. I looked after my company. At that time, being an entrepreneur was a totally different issue to nowadays. To be recognisable as an entrepreneur, that almost led to an obstacle course back then.

When the then president of the Confederation of German Employers (BDA), Hanns Martin Schleyer, was murdered by the Red Army Faction, my wife was at the hairdresser's in Künzelsau. One woman said: "Ah yes, those capitalists, it is only right that they bumped him off!" My wife was horrified and spoke out strongly against this.

You would not hear that any more today, thank God. A lot has changed since then. The majority of the population sees business and companies more positively than the '68 generation. People have a different understanding now. Our economic system is strongly entrenched in the population and valued more highly than back then. That is a paradox that runs parallel to the fully comprehensive state. The zeitgeist at that time was also a long-term effect of World War II and National Socialism. Today, criticism of our economic system is inflamed by the unfathomable global financial transactions. They are threatening to override the political order that our open society set up. Thus liberalism is being weakened from two sides: The expansion of the state with structures that are not transparent is being pitted against the proliferation of financial flows that are seemingly no longer controllable. Both are developments against which our classic image of liberalism appears to be powerless.

Incidentally – what are the '68 generation of that time in comparison? Today they are former Chancellors, mayors, minister-presidents, entrepreneurs – in short, well established and part of our society, generally with a high standard of living. They realised that although business is not everything, everything is nothing without business. Just look at how many of the former '68 generation has shifted sides to business, like former professional demonstrator Joschka Fischer[4].

> *Schleyer was an advocate of the basic idea that individual responsibility is promoted by ownership. He headed a working group in the Confederation of German Employers, "Ownership in the Employee's Hands." Schleyer wanted to enforce that more attention was given in companies to the postulate of opposing communism and the tendency towards a fully comprehensive state that was already becoming apparent at the time through property formation. Schleyer met with huge opposition. Has the awareness been lost among entrepreneurs of the significance of broad distribution of wealth in society?*

There is no lack of insight or perception. But the discussion has focused too much on the topic of company pensions. If property formation is broken down into company pensions, it turns into a highly dangerous topic. I have seen too many companies fail under the costs of company pensions. Look at Lufthansa. That is a catastrophe. Their pension obligations are much too high. But they did not enter them into the balance sheet.

Because they had the option to choose whether they wanted put them into the balance sheet or not. AEG failed due to pension burdens, and many more besides. The mountains of pension obligations that still have to be fulfilled are a huge problem.

I have always resisted this and today I am pleased that I managed to achieve a situation where we have a company pension of moderate, if not to say modest dimensions here in the Group. I have always advocated the principle: We prefer to pay a bit more. That should put the employees in a position to sort out their retirement provisions on their own account. Incidentally, that is also consistent with the principle of subsidiarity.

> *But in Baden-Württemberg, the idea of ownership as the basis for individual responsibility is still very strong…*

But the home ownership rates are not as high as in Spain or Italy. A far higher percentage of the people there own their own house than here in Germany. In Italy and Spain many more citizens own residential property than here in Germany. In Europe, we pretty much bring up the rear here in Germany as regards residential property ownership among private individuals.

> *Statistics! The statistics show a higher rate of ownership for Greece with respect to land and home than for Germany. But when one looks at the houses or the apartments of the majority of the Greeks, then the result is: Such statistics are not comparable with our standards. A quality factor comes into play here.*

Nevertheless, an important social difference is mirrored here. We see in it a standard of living that is oriented less towards state-guaranteed maintenance and more towards self-reliance. However, I am also observing that the trend is moving towards more state throughout Europe, with the exception of the United Kingdom perhaps.

> *Your observations are being superimposed with the widely held perception, often supported by official statistics, that the distribution of wealth is unfair here in Germany. Because people like you are becoming increasingly rich and others who own no capital are continuing to*

fall behind in contrast. Add to this the impression that the so-called middle classes in society are being squashed between rich and poor.

I do not see it like that. It is not true either, Mr Detjen, if you look at the statistics correctly. The rich are indeed getting richer, that is correct. But the middle classes are growing too; it is not as if they are being eliminated. Just a few days ago, the Bundesbank published that Germans are becoming increasingly richer. We were never so rich before overall. Time and again, war and currency reforms put a crimp in that.

Today, there is prosperity in the entire population here in Germany of which the generations before us could only dream. And in addition: In the sweeping statistics about the uneven distribution of wealth, each employee's pension entitlements towards the various pension systems are generally not looked at enough – from the state systems through the occupational pension schemes right up to company pensions. But that is part of each individual's wealth, even if he cannot access it directly or all the time.

And after all, we also know: There is no absolute fairness in this world. Why were you and I born in Germany and not in Ethiopia or Burma or somewhere else? I mean, you can do as much good as you possibly can and give away your entire wealth, but you still won't save the world in doing so. Poverty cannot be eradicated by distributing it more evenly. That is all that would happen if one were to strip the rich of everything and distribute it evenly across the entire world. The problem of poverty in the world must be fought with economic development in the poor countries.

The image of the few who are becoming increasingly richer and the poor who are becoming increasingly numerous is spreading round the world through the media. That will have a political effect. What can those who still believe in the significance of liberalism oppose this with?

Work! There are too many people who always only criticise and pick holes. Often it is the people who do not think for one minute of rolling up their sleeves and knuckling down to work. If this attitude gets the upper hand among politicians, then society will go downhill. Then the most important prerequisite for general prosperity will vanish into oblivion: The principle that prosperity must be earned through work. That everything that is distributed must previously have been earned somewhere. This morning I chuckled as I read in the newspaper about the upcoming mayoral elections in a municipality in Baden-Württemberg. One man had stood for office there who is currently on a cycling tour round Europe and has just returned here from Portugal to do a bit of campaigning. He wants to be elected mayor and then cycle to Portugal again. Of course, people are sensible enough not to elect him. But I see it as a symptom of the state of society that a man like this believes that he is suitable for a responsible position at the head of a municipality.

> *In the world of global financial capitalism, the suggestion that everything that is distributed has to have been earned by work is less than convincing. The big money multiplies without work. Aren't greed and self-interest taking hold in capitalism increasingly unchecked? Let us take the manipulations by banks as an example...*

What many major banks allowed themselves – that can no longer be reconciled with my concept of responsible action. It is not for no reason that many observers used the comparison of a criminal organisation.

> *Even a torch-bearer of liberalism like the Neue Zürcher Zeitung newspaper has repeatedly written that the fundamental ideas of liberalism are being destroyed by the dissolution of boundaries in financial flows and unbridled greed for profit.*

That is why the international efforts to restrict these excesses are so important.

> *Is our economic system not calling itself into question with the manipulations of the financial system, with heedless exploitation of nature and thus of creation?*

The question is whether under global conditions the markets can still solve these problems as one would wish as a liberal and a market economist. World history shows that neither a global empire nor a dynasty has become increasingly richer into the future unchecked. Such developments are stopped somewhere because unforeseen obstacles come up. Wrong decisions, exogenous or internal, can bring about such a stop. Not only

Adolf and Alma Würth with their two sons, around 1949
Photo: Würth company archive

Adolf Würth and his son Reinhold, around 1952
Photo: Würth company archive

First own company building in Künzelsau, 1952
Photo: Würth company archive

The Würth Group headquarters in Künzelsau-Gaisbach today
Photo: Würth company archive

Friendly relationship: Reinhold Würth and photographer Paul Swiridoff
Photo: Roland Bauer, Braunsbach

German President Roman Herzog chatting to Reinhold Würth in 2001
Photo: Würth company archive

Enjoys interaction with many artists, here with Sir Anthony Caro
Photo: Eva-Maria Kraiss, doc bild&text, Schwäbisch Hall

One of the most significant acquisitions on the European art market: The Holbein Madonna is displayed in the Johanniterkirche church in Schwäbisch Hall as the central work of the Old Masters in the Würth collection

Photo: Eva-Maria Kraiss, doc bild&text, Schwäbisch Hall

Reinhold Würth in the Kunsthalle Würth art gallery in Schwäbisch Hall with Georg Baselitz (right), Thaddaeus Ropac (2nd from right), German Chancellor Gerhard Schröder (left) and Werner Spies (2nd from left)

Photo: Eva-Maria Kraiss, doc bild&text, Schwäbisch Hall

Critical eye for quality: Reinhold Würth checks a product from the Würth Line in China
Photo: private

The explorer at the helm of his boat
Photo: private

Reinhold Würth in the spotlight at the Group's major management executives' conference
Photo: andi Schmid, Munich

Reinhold Würth in the company of the Foundation Council of the Foundation for the Promotion of the Reinhold Würth University with Baden-Württemberg Science Minister Theresia Bauer
Photo: Würth company archive

The pilot: Reinhold Würth in the cockpit of his "Falcon"
Photo: andi schmid, Munich

Reinhold Würth with companions at an excavation site in Syria
Photo: Andreas Körner, Stuttgart

At a time when there was no war in Syria yet: Reinhold Würth visiting archaeological excavations which he sponsored
Photo: Andreas Körner, Stuttgart

Protection from the outside – complete overview from the inside
Photo: Andreas Körner, Stuttgart

Reinhold Würth with his daughter Bettina, who is his successor as chair of the Advisory Board
Photo: Würth company archive

The founding father and his wife Carmen Würth
Photo: andi Schmid, Munich

Reinhold and Carmen Würth with their extended family of children, grandchildren and great-granddaughter
Photo: Würth company archive

in business – see Rothschild, see Krupp – but also in politics, see Charlemagne or Napoleon. At some stage, the deck is reshuffled.

Of course I too ask the question: Where is capitalism taking us? Where is the end? Trees cannot grow into the sky; that is quite logical. There are limits to growth, there are limits to wealth in general – but who marks them, who sets them?

Comments

1. FDP: The Free Democratic Party – a liberal German political party which failed to reach the 5% minimum share of the vote to gain any direct seats to the German Bundestag in the 2013 elections for the first time in the party's history.
2. Thomas Dehler was the first German Federal Minister of Justice (1949 to 1953) and as Chairman of the FDP (1954 to 1957) one of the country's most militant liberal politicians in the founding years of the Federal Republic of Germany.
3. Hildegard Hamm-Brücher was a member of the Federal Executive of the FDP for a time and was Minister of State at the Federal Foreign Office from 1976 to 1982.
4. Joschka Fischer: Joseph Martin "Joschka" Fischer, German politician of the alliance Bündnis 90/The Greens party, served as Foreign Minister and Vice Chancellor of Germany from 1998 to 2005. Before entering politics, Fischer was active in the German student movement and left-wing movement (post-)1968 movement (known as "Spontis").

Chapter 5
On the responsibility of the media

Who supervises the watchdogs?

Media are gambling away trust / Why did the call for a new German policy towards Russia receive so little attention?

> *Prejudices against the media in general, and certain newspapers and channels in particular, are widespread in business, even if they are rarely expressed openly. Misunderstandings on both sides are the underlying cause of this. Sometimes it can be heard said that the power of the media has become too large and must be limited. What is your attitude towards the media?*

My critical distance to our media notwithstanding, I appreciate how important free media are for an open society and a democratic state. My critical distance is connected to my understanding of responsibility. There are three starting points for my criticism. Firstly, I all too often see a lack of impartial information in newspapers, radio and television, which instead provide incomplete, biased or even propagandist reports. The most recent example is how public service broadcasters ARD and ZDF ignored the call for a new German policy towards Russia in their most important news broadcasts. Signatories included former German President Roman Herzog and former Chancellor Gerhard Schröder.

Secondly, media presume the right to make prejudgements to which they are not entitled. Anyone who judges others, as the media do frequently and too quickly, has to assume their responsibility publicly. In that sense, I do not think it is enough that newspapers and channels invoke their role as watchdog. Or the increased competition in the media. Who supervises the watchdogs?

Thirdly, with regard to television, and particularly the public-service broadcasters: The wrong role models are being produced for children and young people. A cult of celebrity is being practiced around people who use shows and glamour to lead the young people to believe that life plays out best as entertainment and parties. If at all, achievement is only shown in sports. As to how important hard work in science and research is for our society, for our prosperity – the media hardly impart that at all or not in a way that young people could derive targets from it for their own life decisions.

> *But despite that you surely do not want to subject the media to state supervision or regulation by politicians?*

No. Neither the one nor the other. The media must fulfil their function at their own discretion and competence and with the awareness of their responsibility. This assumes that they do not combine their power with an entitlement to autocracy, that they do not demand more morality and decency of others than of themselves. They should inform in such a way that the citizens can form their own opinions. The public-service broadcasters in particular manipulate their viewers through the selection of information and the manner of portraying events and people. That is why the call for a new German policy towards Russia appeals directly to the media too.

I even experienced the time when there was only the propaganda of the Nazi Reich. As a boy, I experienced first-hand how my father listened to Radio Beromünster, the Swiss foreign broadcaster. That was illegal at the time. Anyone who listened to foreign stations and was caught doing it was punished, often severely. My father used to pull a rug over the radio and over his head so that no one could hear anything outside.

Later there were only the publications of the military government before the Americans permitted the unrestricted freedom of the press in the Basic Law (the German constitution). Today the citizen, the attentive citizen, has a multitude of opportunities to become informed – if he would only use them. You can get your own impression, form your own opinion if you use the many information sources that are literally boundless, geographically and ideologically, on the internet. Yet at the same time the opportunities to manipulate information have increased correspondingly. That is where my scepticism sets in, or one could also say: my mistrust.

Experience and history teach us that political and, admittedly, economic power too always attempts to manipulate people through information. Just think of the quantities of data that are collected by companies of the so-called social media, by Google and not least by the secret services and undoubtedly also used for their various interests. The NSA of the United States is the worst example of this. It is reminiscent of the 19th century, when, before the privacy of correspondence was protected, a secret service agent sat in every small German state and inspected the letters.

How do you personally become informed?

By using a number of sources. I read several German and foreign newspapers every day. On television, I regularly watch the evening news, and on Sundays additionally the Berlin politics programmes afterwards. I have the ZDF app on my mobile. I also use apps to access information sources on the internet. But I am no IT native, more of an IT immigrant. For the formation of an opinion, I find it important to exchange ideas within the family, with entrepreneurs with whom I am friends, with colleagues within the company and with those responsible in public life in the region, in the federal state and in Berlin.

So you are indeed quite well informed?

I am well informed because I use many sources. But how many people do that? Or have as much opportunity to do it as I do? I also notice how differently events and people are portrayed and interpreted in the media. That can be seen positively as an expression of the pluralism in society. But time and again bias or even a deliberate refusal to inform can also be determined. Like now regarding the appeal for a new German policy towards Russia we spoke about, signed by more than 60 figures from public life. Or for example when a newspaper or a channel does not report about an exhibition or an artist who has a big exhibition somewhere. Interests come into play here – competition between cities and art markets, preferences for and aversions against artists, camaraderie between media and art experts.

This phenomenon permeates the entire cultural history. It has nothing to do with the media competition of our time.

It is more effective and weightier when the media have so much influence on so many people as they do in our time. I know, we live in a media society. I also see how the role of the media has changed since the advent of the internet. The competition for attention, for the time that people spend on media, has become stiffer. I observe that in advertising too. Everything is getting louder, often it is actually shrill. Then apparently the temptation is also greater to arouse attention with scandal-mongering.

The media ride the same wave time and again with topics that instil fear because they are not easily understood. The Sunday edition of the Frankfurter Allgemeine Zeitung recently ran a study about how the media addressed the topic of the TTIP negotiations. It reads that TTIP did not receive coverage in the media until the opponents of the free trade agreement with the United States and Canada entered the fray. That gave the opponents the opportunity to move into the foreground in public perception. The media allowed their agenda to be dictated to them, so to speak. That is how programming can take place in voters' heads.

> *Where that occurs, the media abuse their function. They should not allow themselves to be exploited. Not even for what you want.*

It is not a question of my wishes. It always comes back to the old question: Is the glass of water half-full or half-empty? If you always emphasise what is lacking, people's heads will be programmed negatively. You can track that regarding the topic of Europe. In the media, the EU appears more as a bureaucratic monster instead of an oasis of freedom and prosperity in a world that has come off the rails. Maybe the refugees from the Balkans, from Iraq, from Syria and from Africa perceive Europe more realistically than our media.

> *What do you expect then?*

I believe it is the function of the media to inform about the significance of the European Union for our future and to create a good climate for such a task – the expansion of the Union. The press has a huge responsibility in this. That does not work with the recipe: "Bad news is good news, good news is no news."

> *It is not part of the self-image of a free press to place itself at the service of a political mandate. It sees itself as a critical monitor of the protagonists. You are asking too much of the media, dear Mr Würth! The big milestones in German politics were not enforced by the press, but by politicians despite strong headwind from the media. Let us remember Konrad Adenauer and his consistent Western policy, Willy Brandt with his tenacious Eastern policy. After all, it is first and foremost the politicians' task to win majorities for their objectives.*

Of course! But if the media present politics first and foremost as a shambles, if media interpretation and presentation take precedence over information about politics, if what politicians really want is only communicated on the side-lines, then the media simply owe politics a debt; then the media also have to accept responsibility for the failure of politics and not shift the blame onto politics alone.

> *The call for a new German policy towards Russia, which former German President Roman Herzog and former Chancellor Schröder, among others, support, also bears your signature. It criticises "lead writers and commentators" who demonise entire nations. What moved you to sign the appeal?*

I share the concern that bogeymen are being created again, that unilateral recriminations are spreading and that Russia is being squeezed out of Europe. The time has come to warn against this when war is spreading in Ukraine. It is also necessary to remind the media of their obligation. That is why the signatories are calling "on the media to fulfil their duty of impartial reporting more convincingly than up to now." The appeal was not initiated by just anybody. It can be attributed to the previous security advisor to Chancellor Kohl, Horst Teltschik. He participated in a significant role in all the negotiations with the Soviet Union about the reunification of Germany. Let me quote Teltschik, with whom I agree: "Our aim is to give a political signal that the justified criticism of Russia's Ukraine policy does not lead to the progress that we have achieved in the past 25 years in relations with Russia being annulled."

In our media world, where everything is disseminated increasingly faster, irrespective of whether it is true or not, knowledge of history is being lost. However, the conflicts on the fringes of the former Soviet Union have historical roots. That is why the appeal makes the critical statement: "Every journalist versed in foreign policy will understand the Russians' fear since NATO members invited Georgia and Ukraine to become members of the alliance in 2008."

World War I began a hundred years ago. I am not a historian. But I take the warnings of those who know history seriously. There was a lot of discussion about historian Christopher Clark's book "The Sleepwalkers." Clark has compared the current situation in Europe with the conditions before 1914.

No one was capable of creating a blueprint for lasting peace in Europe. In order that Europe does not drift into a war again the way it did back then, the unification of Europe and the establishment of a Russia, including a peace and economic zone, need positive support from the media. I have bemoaned this already in our dialogue about European policy, that the media emphasise more what is not going well and neglect the positive.

> *Even today you accuse the media of creating bogeymen. I see that accusation as too general.*

The fact that there is not just black or white in the world, as the media often suggests, applies here too. All the shades in-between exist too. If one looks into really major politics, the Germans get upset about the human rights violations in China and denounce the system there. But as for the record the United States has – our media do not measure that with the same yardstick. An image of Russia is communicated to us that is concentrated one-sidedly on Putin as the villain. Our media show too little of the different positions that exist in Russian politics and in Russian society too.

Russia is being showcased in the media as the warmonger that wants to rebuild the old Soviet Union. Putin is being blamed as the incarnation of evil. All the blame is being foisted onto him. The Ukraine is being awarded the role of victim. In our television news, we find out little about internal conditions in Ukraine, which is certainly no model for democracy and legal security. We find out little about the economy of Ukraine, which was one of the largest armouries in Europe up to and beyond the end of the Soviet Union – for Russia too.

The fears that arose in Russia because of the eastward expansion of NATO and the attitude of the West in the Ukraine conflict come to light too little in our media. Here in Germany, too, a one-sided propaganda is being practiced and the normal citizen is being programmed, so to speak.

> *Are we not speaking more about Russian state television and its methods now?*

We are speaking about the danger that a propaganda war will follow the dispute that is being waged with weapons in Ukraine. Why was the call for a new German policy towards Russia ignored here in Germany in the most important news programmes of ARD and ZDF? Is that merely coincidence? The call also got lost in the noise in most of the print media, regardless of its prominent signatories from all political camps. Media expert Stefan Niggemeier has revealed how ARD and ZDF made excuses with references to the limited time in the news blocks. In reality, in doing so they actually confirmed the impression that information is manipulated here in Germany too.

Admittedly, Russia is not a role model for independent and objective media. To that extent it can be said that the exhortation to alleviate the people's fear of a new war is also directed to the Russian media. Although it expressly addresses the German media alone, the demand in the appeal also applies to them to give the people a realistic picture of the situation through "responsible reporting based on sound research."

I would like to refer once again to the most recent book by former U.S. Secretary of State Henry Kissinger, who repeatedly points out how the acceleration of the media drives politics and thus prevents reflection. The new ways of relaying information faster and networking it, making it available everywhere, cause conflicts to escalate, get out of control and lose transparency, instead of creating transparency. That is what Kissinger says. That is being played out in relation to Russia. Our media are not making Russia more comprehensible to us, but are conveying a prejudiced picture.

If you travel around in Russia, you can observe how unbelievably friendly, hospitable and obliging the people are. It is imperative to remain fair here and observe things from both sides. When do our media ever report on live in Vladivostok, in Archangelsk, in Irkutsk – meaning from the parts of Russia which in our imagination are far away? And what do we find out about the young people at the universities, about their dreams and desires? Russia is more than Putin.

Everyone must become informed from as many sources as possible. The internet offers many opportunities to do this – here in Germany and fortunately also for the Russians. Thus they are not solely reliant on Russian state television. They can also become informed from external sources.

> *Does your mistrust towards the media also stem from your experience in connection with your criminal tax proceedings?*

I had a bad experience. If you are in a situation like that, you get the impression that the entire press is lashing out at you regardless of the consequences. Then you suddenly don't have a good side any more, you are just a crook and a gangster. But I never had one cent of illegal income.

During the time in question, I gave more than €40 million in donations. Not a mention of that appeared in the press, although it was well-known. That was hushed up. No research was carried out. No one asked the question: Why should someone who gives €40 million in donations over two years at the same time evade taxes? That does not fit at all, it is absurd.

Instead, a person like this is pilloried. The media appear to have taken over the function of the pillory in our time, whether of their own volition or through interference by interested parties. It certainly cannot be a coincidence that the media, including television, are already standing outside the house when the tax investigators move in on prominent businesspeople! One has to ask if there is sometimes a camaraderie between judiciary and media. One does not have to condone what skeletons the person concerned in this case has in their cupboard, and less so what the president of Bayern Munich[1] perpetrated. But it is going too far if people are pilloried in the media simply because there are grounds for suspicion before justice is done in the particular case.

> The media should not let themselves be exploited as a pillory. But it is their function to uncover wrongdoings. Too many scandals – for example the Landesbanks, Hypo Alpe Adria, Berlin Airport, ADAC, etc.[2] – would have stayed under wraps if publicity had not been created for them through the media.

Yes, that is ok! But the media have to stick to the facts. What do we experience time and again instead? Speculations and suspicions are presented like facts, opinion mixed with report, apparently only so that copy sales or ratings are achieved. Then the one media source refers to the others, they mutually quote one another as if this could turn prejudices into facts. Quality journalism is spoken about so often. Is it not right and proper then, that where reasons actually do exist for suspicion of criminal offences and this is justifiably reported, that the exonerating aspects should also be presented to readers and viewers?

Comments

1. The president of German football team Bayern Munich, Uli Hoeness, was given a jail sentence after being convicted of tax fraud in 2014, whereupon he stepped down from his post.
2. In the scandals listed here which were uncovered by the media, it was a case of public mismanagement (for example within the Landesbanks) or of misconduct on the part of management and on the supervisory boards (for example within the ADAC, or Allgemeiner Deutscher Automobil-Club, a German roadside assistance association which has almost 19 million members).

Chapter 6
Commercial traveller, pilot, mariner, hiker

Philosophy of life: Vibrant Curiosity

Travel makes up for university / The idiom of home *(Heimat)* indicates character / On the poetry of flying into the sunrise

> *In the autobiographical sections of your publications, you write about the beginning of your professional career primarily in the form of sales trips. You describe how you bought your first car, then a plane, to expand your sphere of activity. Your descriptions clearly indicate passion for selling. Is your occupation as travelling salesman what is known in the classic meaning as a commercial traveller?*

My father took me out of secondary school before I could get as far as the Abitur, the school leaving examination. He showed me the business – and that was primarily sales. He took me with him on his trips, as far as Switzerland. In 1952, he sent me on a sales trip alone for the first time. I stayed in Düsseldorf for two weeks and visited customers in the city and as far as Wuppertal. One of the first customers in Düsseldorf was VW dealer Adalbert Moll. The purchasing manager looked me over keenly through his glasses. He gave me one of the first orders – brass-chromed 6 x 15 and 6 x 20 number plates for VW Transporters. Thus I really learned to sell from scratch. And found I enjoyed it right from the start.

Travelling was always connected to selling. My father had constantly expanded our market already – to the extent that travel options improved after the war. But because my father had no driving licence, he successfully applied for a special permit for me so that I could already take my driving licence at the age of sixteen instead of at eighteen. Beforehand I had to have my physical fitness tested twice by the state health department. I do not know any more if it was a sunny day when I received the grey document on linen paper – but my mood was like a sunny spring day. This document has accompanied me around the world up to the present day – from Patagonia to Japan, from Spitzbergen to Ushuaia, from New York to Tomsk or Xian. But the boy in the photo no longer matches the grey-haired man I am today at all...

> *Was your enjoyment of travel more than a lucky coincidence? The commercial traveller has meantime become a world traveller.*

Travel is life, life is travel. To me, that is an equation that cannot be split up. I simply cannot sit around at home. A week in the daily routine at home passes like lightning. But when I travel, the impressions of one week are so diverse that it seems like months have passed since I left home.

> *Are you a restless spirit?*

At least that is what my wife says…

> *So you are a commercial traveller and a globetrotter? Travel as a diversion from boredom in daily life?*

Boredom is foreign to me. I am not a globetrotter either. My business travel is my focus. Even today, I am sometimes out with the sales force, meaning, participating in selling to customers. In the 65 years I have been working in my profession since 1949, I have travelled millions of kilometres to all corners of the world. The idea behind it was always to tap new markets. If the market is expanded, the travel and the selling always become more interesting. Even today, I am travelling for almost half the year. To me, selling is and will remain the nicest profession.

> *Why?*

I was in Sweden just two weeks ago. We were inaugurating a new plant there. I took the opportunity of being there to visit customers. I was up already at five in the morning and had left the hotel at twenty to seven with a salesperson so that we could be visiting the first customer by seven. I still enjoy that today; it is great fun. It has always given me incredible pleasure to communicate with people, to observe people, to get to know people.

In the decades in which I have now been in this job, I have been able to acquire good knowledge of human nature in sales. One gets to know the gestures, the facial expressions, one gets to know that little twitch of the eyes or the cheeks and can draw many conclusions from it. That is how one learns to read people well. That is also important for sales. Because of this opportunity to communicate with people, the profession of salesperson, of travelling salesperson, is the nicest of all.

> Today, almost half of your approximately 66,000 employees work in sales. How has the occupational profile changed compared to the time you started in the job?

A lot has changed. Today, the salesperson has to have a lot more knowledge of his customers' market. More advisory expertise is required of him. The markets are changing faster than before because of globalisation and because of innovation in technology. Customers have to be supplied faster, if possible on the same day that they place their order. That only works with modern electronic instruments and organisational structures. All of this requires much more sales training than before. The company must enable more occupational training, the salesperson has to muster up greater willingness to learn.

I can explain this in concrete terms for my company, for our sector. In former times, we used to work a lot with original samples and sample cards. Then the catalogues came later. Today, everything is done on tablet computers. The tools of the trade of a sales rep have changed immensely. That changes the sales strategies, the sales organisation, the warehousing and the despatch. That is a huge challenge for a company that was based on the traditional sales structures.

I have always ensured, both in my own case and that of the sales employees, that time is used as efficiently as possible. Initially, I could not get into these iPad computers at all. I soon learned that the previous computers did not achieve the capabilities that these tablets provide today. Furthermore, they were slower. My change of heart is linked to the perfection of the technology that gives the salesperson more time to serve the customers. We have to use technology with this in mind. Many people think, now we soon won't need any salespeople any more, that will just all happen electronically. That is a fallacy. We will also need the people who maintain personal contact with the customers.

> *You emphasise in your papers on entrepreneurship how important it is to provide material incentives to reward success. But you also sometimes write angry letters to the salespeople. Do the two belong together – carrot and stick?*

Not in the way that you mean! And I really do not like your word "stick" at all. Rewards and performance requirements belong together, because there are very different characters of people. Some can only be motivated by money; for others, money only plays a minor role. You have to find the concept for each person that ultimately produces the required performance for the company, according to the individual capabilities and preferences. In sales, you need a knowledge of human nature on both sides – on the customer side and one-to-one among the sales force. Metaphorically speaking: If you have to deal with thirty thousand salespeople, then you will find the most diverse types of people among them, everything that walks on God's green earth, so to speak – the braggarts, the uncommunicative, the hot-tempered, the sanguine and all the other types of people there are.

The material incentives are no longer a priority for an increasingly large percentage of the sales reps; they pursue immaterial values in their lives too. Then providing incentives has no relevance. They do not care about such incentives. You have to communicate differently with these employees than with those who are focused first and foremost on money. In such a large organisation like our sales division, you cannot personalise to such an extent that you say to each person precisely the word that is appropriate to him individually.

Then it can happen that the person who is not interested in money at all is confronted with a speech that is actually addressing those who are responsive to bonuses – and vice versa. Then you have to expect a modicum of tolerance and broad-mindedness from the employees concerned too.

> *What impressions have you discovered on your sales trips?*

There is a reason why it is said that travel educates. After all, during my training I did not see one university. My university, so to speak, was the travelling. For example, you will get no better geography lesson than when you travel and observe closely. Then you do not have to spend time on photos and books and descriptions. You see and experience landscapes, places, rivers and lakes, not to mention the different breeds of people. Dealing with people educates too. You get new perspectives. Travel conveys impressions and shapes our thinking. With these experiences, I feel I am a European and a world citizen.

My trips have made me more tolerant than average – in all directions, to all parts of the world, cultural groups, religions. I view this diversity of cultures and religions with respect and with understanding. Last summer, I was in Alaska and Canada and was interested in the culture of the Inuit – those are the indigenous people there. Originally, they had no writing system. But they created other forms of expression with which they gave their culture shape in the most literal sense of the word. This was the origin of the five-metre-high totem poles, which portray earthly existence and the Inuits' belief in their hereafter extremely impressively.

> *You have grown beyond being an entrepreneur from Hohenlohe and become a global player with your Group. As a person too?*

I attribute my success to a few characteristics in which elements of my native origins can also be spotted: diligence, perseverance, tenacity, energy and the ability to win over and inspire people and lead them to achieve goals. Former German President Heuss characterised the people of Hohenlohe as: "bright, vigorous, vivacious, a little self-opinionated and self-assured." It did me good that I got out of the Hohenlohe environment at an early stage too, and later got around the entire world.

If you wish, you can differentiate between my personal interests and my entrepreneurial activities. But the two belong together and can never be separated completely. One must know the markets where the Group operates worldwide. Markets are not just statistical economic entities. However much the markets are also becoming more alike in a globalised world, because people's needs are ultimately the same or similar everywhere – large differences still remain. They have their origins in the specific conditions of the markets that have developed out of the historical diversity of continents, states and ethnic structures.

All of that has always fascinated me; it drew me out into the world. When my client base was still limited to my home *(Heimat)* of Hohenlohe, I knew:

There is more of the world over the hill, there is still a lot to be discovered there. In order to turn a regional trading company into a corporate group with global reach, one has to also participate personally as a global player.

> *Is globalisation a key to creating a more peaceful world? True to the motto: "Whoever is trading with one another will not shoot at one another?"*

Definitely! Nowadays, world trade is not primarily exploitation, but rather helps to maintain peace. World trade creates a balance of wealth in the world, at least in low percentages. It promotes understanding among people. Even apparently trivial phenomena contribute to this, for example technical products that must be usable everywhere in the world, in the facilities of power stations or in the motor vehicle industry. Anyone who always deals with this has to acquire a common understanding of technology, right up to understanding operating instructions. In the end of the day, all countries want to have a share in technological advances. They can do that better in a peaceful exchange of trade than where conflicts, or even wars divide the people and the markets.

Let us look at the Ukraine crisis. I am sure that President Putin has understood that the sanctions are of no benefit to him and that ultimately his position as a politician in Russia, from the citizens' viewpoint, will be weakened if the conflict drags on. Russia is actually more likely to achieve an improvement in its citizens' economic situation through global collaboration in trade than if the immense burdens continue to rise for Crimea and Ukraine. After all, billions will have to be pumped into them to keep the economy going.

> *Does the old British motto still apply, that trade follows the flag?*

I do not think so. Nowadays, trade has become international. Trade follows the profit opportunities and not the flag.

> *How important to you is the planned trade agreement with the United States (TTIP), which is highly controversial?*

That may bring us some advantages, but those are pretty negligible for our Group. Disadvantages could arise for us if we were showered with genetically modified foodstuffs in Europe. But the negotiations have not really begun yet. On the other hand, I see the opportunities for business on both sides of the Atlantic. If I were to be asked right now, do you support it or do you oppose it, I would say +2 on a scale of −10 to +10. But no more. For the Würth Group, the EU is by far the most important trade area.

> We determined earlier that trade is an element that contributes to the establishment of peace in the world. But that definitely does not apply to the arms trade. It is a branch of industry that is not to be underestimated, even in Germany.

I do of course advocate that the sale of weapons to private individuals must be strictly forbidden. The EU should assume responsibility for this, and we should have a European office for granting export licenses for arms. Because that plays a role in the competition between France, Germany and the UK and jobs are at issue, the national governments are always in a quandary. Then they all close their eyes down to the last person when business is going to Qatar or Saudi Arabia. Arms should really be eliminated. The manufacture of arms should simply be forbidden, worldwide.

> That is wishful thinking…

If we no longer have such wishes, then we no longer believe that we have a responsibility for our future generations and should create a better world.

> When you are on trips round the world as a travelling salesman on company business, how important are the German economic representatives in embassies, foreign chambers of commerce, representative offices of the federal states to you then?

Hmm.

> I should have guessed I would get this answer…

I have never needed a German consulate or an embassy. Nowadays, I occasionally receive invitations from the ambassador when I am abroad, like last year in Sri Lanka. Those are usually pleasant diversions. The diplomatic service has its own conventions. To put it bluntly: Diplomats form a party set consisting of national holidays, days of remembrance, ministerial visits, official functions and other occasions where there are cocktails. When states are dealing with one another, this sort of thing is evidently necessary in the capital cities. But I also ask myself: Why do we need 28 embassies from all EU states in Washington nowadays, when we are actually supposed to make a unified appearance as the EU? The states could save billions there. After all, we also have a big EU representative office in Washington. The problem is that the national legislative processes are still too different in some areas of the EU.

The shift in the production facilities of important goods is a far-reaching consequence of globalisation. How is that affecting the Würth Group?

Not particularly. We were directly affected by solar technology, where a large portion of production moved to the countries in the low-cost regions. Of course there are sectors for whom that was fundamental, for example for so-called brown goods, meaning radio and television appliances, or for the manufacture of cameras. Do many people today still remember that Germany was once the leading camera manufacturer?

If one sees this development from a broader perspective, it does help, as I have already said at another juncture, to equalise quality of life in the world. The more manpower China needs, the faster wages will rise there, even dramatically. That is ok. It will contribute to maintaining internal peace there.

In comparison to the other continents, Africa is far behind in its economic development. What connections do you, the traveller, have with Africa, what does the Group have?

We are only represented with our own company in Kenya and South Africa. I find the development in Angola very striking. Africa in general is underestimated all too often. According to global economic statistics, Africa as a continent currently has enormous economic growth percentage-wise. This is particularly due to the exploitation of raw materials. It is almost spooky how fast China's investments in Africa have grown. China is acquiring mining rights, building roads and railways on a large scale. That creates the impression that Africa is largely in Chinese hands.

In the 19th century, Germany made a huge drive for colonies in Africa. What role do you see for Germany in Africa today?

I see no major obligation there, except in Namibia. I have travelled a lot in Namibia. The marks that were made there in German colonial times are still very visible today. I was surprised time and again how often I was addressed in German. German development aid has contributed a lot to stability in Namibia. Clever politics has led to a situation where farmers were rarely dispossessed there as occurred in other former colonies. That is also promoting Namibia's stability.

A few years ago, you had a large Group conference in South Africa. Did you want to direct the management executives' attention to Africa by doing this?

That was definitely one intention that we pursued when we decided on Cape Town. There are other reasons for this too. We want to hold congresses like this for several hundred employees in places that are attractive and cost-effective. We also give managers and their wives the opportunity to add on a few days' holiday beforehand or afterwards. South Africa is ideally suited for this. It was a huge success at the time and broadened the horizons of all participants.

Travelling salesman Würth has turned into an educational tourist?

That is what my grandchildren maintain, at least. When they travel with me, they sometimes already say in the morning: "Grandpa, I have museum allergy and church allergy today, I cannot come with you on the sightseeing tour."

You always have your camera with you when you travel. You have given lectures about your trips, an exhibition with photographs and published an illustrated book with your pictures of Asia. Are there more to follow?

I could fill volumes with my photos and notes. I made the illustrated books primarily for the family. Photography can be regarded as my hobby. I started already as a twelve-year-old with a box camera – that was a kind of everyman's camera that cost five marks at the time. In the meantime, I have taken tens of thousands of photos that are also archived, catalogued and managed. A young photographer I have employed on a part-time basis deals with that.

I can use the camera to record impressions and take them home with me. From time to time, I take the photographs out of the archive to mull over my impressions of the trip, reflect on them. When business commitments dominate on the weekdays of my trips, I use the weekends to get more indepth impressions. I also use the recordings I make in a kind of diary during my trips for this.

In 2006, I held the first photo exhibition in Künzelsau at our Group's headquarters. An illustrated book "Asien im Sucher" (Asia in the Viewfinder) was published to go with it. I could publish many more photo books too, from my trips from Argentina to Siberia. It gives me pleasure to allow others to participate in my impressions.

What encounters left the strongest impressions on you?

I cannot describe my experiences as well as Johann Gottfried Seume has achieved in his travel diary, "Stroll To Syracuse In The Year 1802." Back then, in 1802, Italy was a largely unknown country for central Europeans. Seume wrote his impressions realistically and critically. No one can do it like that anymore – and with photos, videos and personalised books there are many more forms of expression for travel experiences.

I cannot create a hierarchy of travel impressions. The impressions are too diverse – and yet together have a combined effect. They stick, and often suddenly and unexpectedly come very much alive again. That stretches back to my childhood. In 1950, I was on a business trip and holiday to northern Germany with my parents. We drove in our family's first car, a 1937 Opel Olympia we had bought used. Repairs had to be made constantly. My mother had prepared the provisions for our journey, wrapped in cellophane. Around Hannoversch Münden the motorway bridge was still destroyed. When we drove over the Elbbrücken bridges into the city of Hamburg, saw the ships, the big, wide world opened up for me for the first time. When I saw the Baltic Sea later, I was simply speechless. It seemed to me like an endless mountain.

I experienced the exoticism of faraway worlds for the first time in 1962, when my wife and I took our first long-distance trip. We flew to Osaka to the world exhibition. Today, a trip to Japan is definitely nothing special. Back then, when we ordered two flight tickets to Tokyo and Osaka at the travel agent's, it was a minor sensation.

Places that draw crowds of tourists today remain very individual as an experience, depending on oneself. I delight in the privilege of not having to move in the tourist hordes but be able to put together and implement my own programme.

The magnificent structures in China are unforgettable, the contrast between the old colonial buildings on the Bund in Shanghai and the sky-scraping high-rise buildings in Pudong – we have nothing comparable to that in Europe. The temples in Angkor impressed me deeply, the aesthetic of decline and maintained culture in which a fascinating religious cosmos is revealed, mysterious and captivating in its beauty.

There are other types of unforgettable impressions. Great impressions do not have to be exotic. I once used to do a bit of mountaineering. My most important experience as an alpinist was climbing the Cinque Torri, the five towers in the Dolomites. We were a seven-man rope team, went up there and then abseiled down the 300- to 400-metre-high vertical wall. For my South Tyrolean friends, that was tame. For me, it was a huge event. Halfway down, we had to swing around on the rope in such a way that we could reach a path. One person was abseiled too far down, got stuck on the wall and had to be pulled up again. For the South Tyrolean pros a routine task, for me exciting to the tips of my fingers.

Another experience, a hike at and into the Grand Canyon, will remain imprinted on my memory in every detail for a lifetime – partly because I had so many blisters on my feet from walking. I was at the Grand Canyon with my wife. There is a warning in every hotel room there: "Caution. Please do not attempt to go down and up again in one day." And what did I do? 1,900 metres down and up again! We did not set off immediately at four or four thirty in the morning either, but not until eight thirty. We took ice cubes along for the wine and everything imaginable for the picnic – down as far as the Colorado River. Then up again! And I was an idiot; I only put on one pair of socks, although as a proficient hiker I should have known that I should have put on two pairs at least. When we got back to the hotel again at eight thirty in the evening, we were absolutely shattered. You get five climate zones on this track. Down below, it was so hot and dry that I thought my tongue was a piece of swollen meat.

> *I met you in Bayreuth as a hiker; on days with no performances or before the concerts, you went to the Fichtelgebirge mountains. You fly, you sail – but you still go hiking too. Is hiking the counterpart to the speed that sets the pace on business trips? The slowness of walking as a contrast?*

I have never viewed it like that. Hiking is nice. You experience impressions much more intensively than with any other type of movement; even on a bicycle you do not see as much as when you are walking. The subtlety of the impressions declines as the speed increases; that is quite normal. When you hike, then you see the butterfly that is perched on the flower, or a little rock formation that you cannot discern when you travel by car or by airplane.

> *Is this converging on the integration of man into nature?*

I find that is too easy to misunderstand. I am not esoteric. Such an approach does not suit me. I am not a philosopher. The answer to your question is quite simple: I have always enjoyed going walking, I have always liked to go on hikes and it was also interesting. Encounters with nature can also proceed rationally. Maybe the rational has become part of my nature because I am a businessman. Or conversely: I became a businessman because the rational is in my nature? Maybe you will understand that better if I say to you: I always have a map with me; if I am somewhere without a map, or a city map, I am only half a person. That is always very important. I need verifiable orientation.

> *Was it like that even before the flying?*

It was certainly reinforced by the flying. It was always important to me to know how I get to where. If you hike in an unfamiliar area, then you want to know: Can I do a circuit or do I have to return by the same route? You can only decide that if you have a map.

> *Your trips have also taken you into academic worlds, although you never went to university. Did you experience the universities as another world, as a contrast to your entrepreneurial world?*

Not really. All the worlds we live in are inter-dependent in manifold ways. To the same extent that the continents are connected in manifold ways today and we travel round the world globally, in the same way science is also linked closely to practical application in business. The scientist and researcher no longer work in an ivory tower. Today, everyone is definitely much more aware of their mutual dependence than before. This interdependence tears down the class distinctions in society between academic, craft and even service work that appears highly trivial. Even the Nobel prizewinner cannot do without the refuse collectors. In the same way, the refuse collector could not buy himself a flat-screen television if the scientists did not exist to invent it. To that extent, the world is a closed entity. All participants contribute their part to keep the whole going. I do not want to make this differentiation between science and unscientific activities any more.

> *Are there travel destinations that you visit time and again? Places whose fascination has never left you?*

To me, Venice always had a very special splendour. The Kruger National Park constantly draws me. New York and Shanghai are also places that have a magical effect on me. They are new each time you come back again. You want to see once again what impressed you so much on your first visit, and immediately you are captured by new things. The momentum of change is just staggering.

> *Do you still have a terra incognita? White areas on your world map?*

Yes, many of course; for example, I have never been to the Antarctic. Then there are still many countries in Africa where I have not yet been, those countries that are immediately to the north and to the south of the Equator. In that area, I have only travelled in Kenya so far. Of course, that is always related to political situations. Where there is unrest, you do not necessarily have to go there. There is no market to develop there either.

Is the Antarctic beckoning?

Since I have got to know Alaska, that is to say, the Arctic ice world, the Antarctic no longer exerts such a pull over me. But I have read a lot about the Antarctic continent and the research stations that are there from many countries. In fact, we also have a German Antarctic station. I listened to Reinhold Messner tell about his Antarctic expedition. We were one of his sponsors when he did his huge traverse of the South Pole on skis – a few thousand kilometres.

> *Does the particular attraction of the Antarctic lie in the fact that it is the only continent that has not yet been exploited with no regard for nature?*

But not for long. It is going to start very quickly, that the natural resources are exploited there.

> *Is it our fate that we humans translate the divine order, "Subdue the earth," into exploitation?*

I do not know. But it is true: We manage the Starship Earth. What will happen to humanity in future, no one knows. In cosmic history, humanity is a second-long event. And we may only be around for one more second; but whether that will be another thousand years or another twenty thousand years, that is totally irrelevant. It is zero in the events of the cosmos.

> *Management covers many possibilities: sensible management, preservation, sustainable management or even destruction.*

Do you know, the term sustainable management sounds good. Particularly in political speeches. But what happens in practice is still a completely different story, unfortunately. Who is really prepared to take all the consequences that would ensue if sustainability was really made the guiding principle? Who actually thinks about how much oil is used for the manufacture of plastic? Every litre that we burn in the car as petrol; that will never come back. Who actually knows that the energy footprint of an electric car, if you include its manufacture, is worse than that of a diesel car?

The term sustainability is abused too much. In the end, solar energy will probably remain our must sustainable source. Maybe we will also be able to use wood in the future – after all, sustainability comes from the forestry industry.

I find the question of what is going to happen to humanity in future infinitely more important than the question of how global trade is going to develop or what will become of capitalism.

After all, those are just trifles in the end of the day compared to the big question about the future of mankind which we have to tackle today. Let us think about the demographics. Let us think about genetics, about the use of technology and electronics in the media. Then we see how people can be manipulated – physically and mentally. The discussions about assisted suicides and population control show us quite clearly that humanity is getting ready to become absolute masters of life and death.

Stephen Hawking said that humanity only has one chance to survive, by enabling itself to settle on another planet. And he was actually right too. Humanity is increasing in overall numbers at such a rate that you have to ask: Where is this supposed to end – ten billion, twelve billion, twenty billion? Sometime the Earth will be full – and what then? In the past, wars solved these kinds of problems – decimated the population. We are facing the challenge of accomplishing that peacefully.

> Hawking sees the expansion into space as an opportunity not only for settlement but also for resources.

But it is so unlikely that this will be achievable! The distances in space are so immense, and the next star is outside our solar system. Fifty or a hundred light years away. The fastest travel speed is the speed of light, at least, as far as we still know today – and that is the breaking point. Even if our metabolism slows down so much at the speed of light and you could maybe live for thousands of years. That makes my expectations for the future of mankind tend to be pessimistic.

Is your boat a place of inspiration, of relaxation? A place where you can take time for your family and for meeting friends?

Yes, it is indeed a little quieter then on the boat than in my everyday working life, but not much. When we are close to shore, then sightseeing tours are the order of the day. Every day, I get stacks of post via the internet which I answer. Then I have to dictate. I also study the travel guides for our excursions to the sights on shore, mostly historical places. Every morning, I get the day's newspapers, F.A.Z., Welt, Handelsblatt, Neue Zürcher Zeitung; we have a newspaper printer on board. The day passes much too fast.

So, like your wife says, always a restless spirit?

Yes! It is well known that I was always very inquisitive. Curiosity automatically means restlessness, because you want to know what is happening around you, what is happening around the corner, what is happening tomorrow.

Your yacht is called "Vibrant Curiosity." Is that your life motto?

One of them anyway. I invented the name. Every year or every second year, we have a motto in the Group on which we concentrate. It is something similar to the "Thought for today." Years ago, I chose "Vibrant Curiosity" as the annual motto for the company. I wanted to use it to express that the entire company is inquisitive and champing at the bit to set off time and again towards new goals. I liked it so much that I adopted the motto as the name of the boat. Everyone who devotes themselves to seafaring says: That is a very beautiful name.

Do you still have the travel bug?

Not really. Travel has also become routine for me in the course of my life.

But where is the vibration in the curiosity then?

You don't need the travel bug for that! Your head does not function at its best when you have a high fever and are in the delirium of fever. Vibration can also stem from delight. Curiosity is also looking forward to new things. Experiencing excitement, history, like recently in Avignon in the

Papal Palace and in the Hotel d'Europe, where Napoleon and Hemingway once stayed.

> *You started flying for business reasons. But travel is also a sensual experience. After all your travel experiences, are you still receptive to the sensuality of travel?*

Of course I am still receptive to sensuality. Beauty is always an enthrallment, not just the beauty of people. Pictures of cities have their own aesthetic allures, as do the works of the fine arts. I have a lot of time for beauty.

> *Reinhold Würth the aviator with an air transport pilot licence – does he still feel a little of the passion for flying that we know from Antoine de Saint-Exupéry?*

Do you know, this sensuality is always there. Right from the moment when you are standing in front of the plane. You feel the harmony of technologies and characteristics with which a machine like this is designed. This is a perfection of technology and form that, despite its expression of masculine power, has something feminine about it too. When you take these thirty tonnes into the air and push the throttle forward – that is a vibrating experience every time.

> *To quote Reinhard Mey's song: "Above the clouds, the freedom must be unlimited?"*

It isn't. You are stuck in the cockpit.

> *No particular feelings of freedom?*

Sometimes, certainly. Let me describe that specifically. When I was in Alaska last year, we took two day-trips, one from Juneau to Anchorage and one from Juneau to Kodiak. And when we were flying back from Kodiak in the late afternoon, that would be eastward then, the sun was halfway to the left behind us, and halfway to the left in front of us was Alaska's gigantic glacier world, glittering and gleaming from the sun we had behind us. That was of course a captivating experience. Even on the flight from Europe to Alaska we had – something that is very rare – cloudless weather below us over Greenland. We were up at forty thousand feet and could almost touch this Greenlandic ice desert below us with our hands. There were little lakes of meltwater in the ice made by the sun.

We could also see the consequences of climate change in this. Then huge impressions turn into triggers for reflection, for asking questions about how we treat the Earth that has been entrusted to us.

An enthrallment also occurs every time when you fly eastwards through the night and the sun rises. This is imprinted on my memory particularly from a trip during which we flew from Auckland in New Zealand to Papeete in the Pacific. We took off at eleven in the evening local time. That was a marvellous night – cloudless, the moon shone brightly in the black sky, below us the gleaming Pacific, the moon was mirrored in the dark sides, and then towards morning, initially very delicately, just a thin, pale streak. That was followed shortly afterwards by turquoise and pink. Then, when the sun slowly comes over the horizon, then the high cloudscapes already start to come between them. The moon is still there, but increasingly wanes. Those are flying experiences that stay with you for a lifetime.

> *That sounds like a poetry of flying.*

Yes, that is how I perceive these experiences. If I was talented as a writer, then I would write a little essay about it. Or maybe a poem…

> *Writing begins with writing…*

Decades ago, I promised myself: When I retire, I will write a crime novel. Up to now, I have lacked the time to do it. Maybe someone like me, who has found his calling as a travelling salesperson, is not suited to being a pensioner…

> *What impressions did art collector Reinhold Würth take back with him from his travels? Is what you have stored in your head from the world reflected in your collection?*

On my travels, I regularly visit art museums. I learned a lot from that. Occasionally, I have asked in the museums for the addresses of artists who are still alive and then acquired one or other of their works if I liked something particularly well. I have also repeatedly had surprising impressions and then incorporated artists I did not know at all into the collection.

I remember one case in New York. We went walking there in Greenwich Village and we saw works by an English artist in a gallery display window. They fascinated me straight away. That was a type of object art, three-dimensional pictures. Now I am thinking about making a monographic exhibition out of it sometime. When you walk over and back in front of pictures like this, doors open up. Of course, that is viewed with disdain by the greats of the art expert world. But I do not care. I like to be impressed by art in my own way. The arrogance of the professional experts can be seen in the example of Niki de Saint Phalle; she was initially completely rejected. And now she is admired worldwide, her sculpture park in Tuscany attracts art lovers from around the world.

> *What impression did the encounter with non-European art have on you? You know the influence that Polynesian and African art had on the fine arts here in Europe in the 20th century. Were you able to retrace the development itself?*

The art of primitive peoples impressed me greatly. I had previously known many works by Picasso, and was then surprised time and again by how close he is to Native Art. One formative experience for me was the "Primitivism in 20th Century Art" exhibition in the Museum of Modern Art in New York in 1984. Particularly the juxtaposition of a Picasso sculpture with a sculpture from Polynesia stuck in my mind. That was almost spooky. One to one! But the experts are one hundred percent certain that Picasso could never have seen the sculpture from the South Seas. That is how we discover a universal memory among humanity.

Another intense experience was the encounter with Horst Antes – he makes these *Kopffüßler* (literally translated, "head footers," figures without necks, and very little chest and stomach). The Pueblo Indians were making comparable figures long beforehand. Irrespective of whether Antes knew them or not when he started on his enigmatic beings – it can also be seen from this that phenomena repeat themselves in human and art history. That is particularly pronounced in the forms of expression that people make of themselves in art.

> *Have you yourself collected the art of other peoples that can be designated "primitivism"?*

We have African art in my private collection. But that is not very significant. I took on this collection from an art dealer in Salzburg, exhibited it partially on my boat, some of it is in Salzburg in my library. There are very nice things in it.

> *You travel around the world, but constantly call Hohenlohe your home (Heimat), where you also regularly find the focal point of your life close to the Group headquarters. How important is a home with a geographical connection still today? Are we all turning into "hommes nomades," as the former French minister Jacques Attali described modern man? Is that what the refugees are who come to us from Africa, Afghanistan, Syria, Iraq, because they are seeking security and work here?*

Home *(Heimat)* in the traditional definition is declining in importance. Today people are whirled through countries and continents – for work, in the wake of tourism, through migration, displacement and escape. If you then talk to these people, then many in the second generation no longer know where they came from. At best only family ties remain.

We should not just complain about the loss of the old bonds, but welcome the gain we have made in people through migration and globalisation. We should strive to win the people who come to us as refugees for our society and empower them to collaborate on our future. People only feel at home in the long run in the place where they feel comfortable, where they have security for their families and work; that is where they set up the focal point of their lives.

There is a small column in the Salzburger Nachrichten newspaper about foreigners who live in Salzburg: How do you feel here? The majority of the people say: My home *(Heimat)* is here, because I have the focal point of my life here.

Hohenlohe feels like home to me and I experience this emotional dimension as something that is very nice. My wife's emotional connection is even stronger. She has become heavily involved with the Anne-Sophie-Hotel and with friends here. That is a connection to Hohenlohe for me too.

However, I also like living in Salzburg. Maybe I would have moved there completely, made it my main residence, if it was not for my wife. Then I would simply have my main residence in Salzburg nowadays and would feel incredibly at home there. To me, Salzburg is not just my second home *(Heimat)*, but sometimes my first.

> *Language is also part of one's emotional home (Heimat). What role does it play for you? You cultivate the Hohenlohe accent. You also participated in the Baden-Württemberg advertising campaign with the statement: "We are capable of everything, apart from High German."*

I see it as a strong and positive character trait if someone maintains his parlance. I have never made a secret of the fact that I come from Hohenlohe. I have never attempted to acquire the Salzburg dialect so that the people there do not notice that I am not a native.

I always admired the same attitude in my stepfather. My mother got married a second time, of course, to Walter Kindermann; he was from Westphalia, a tax officer, and managed the tax office in Künzelsau. Up to the day he died, he spoke crystal-clear Westphalian. Although he spent more than thirty years here in Hohenlohe, not one Hohenlohe sound could be heard in his speech. I found that very nice.

> *What is so attractive, so special about Salzburg?*

My family has two lovely properties in a beautiful setting in Salzburg. The city exudes an endearing harmony. The cultural diversity is very appealing too. You will hardly find a second comparable place in Europe with so much culture in one spot like in Salzburg – the whole year round. The museums are highly appealing. The nature museum is one of the leading museums of its kind in the world. Where does an art museum have such an attractive location as the one up on the hill in Salzburg? Medical care is excellent, particularly the university clinic.

> *Does the social life in Salzburg play an important role for you?*

A subordinate one. I am not part of the in-crowd, neither is my wife. We do not shove our way into the places where those people appear who are known as the beautiful people. We invite people to come to our home a few times a year. Those are four, five events per year. Most of the invitations we receive, I decline them. You can get two, three invitations for the same evening. I don't play those types of games. I have a lot to do and am happy when I have a few hours' peace in Salzburg – or time to stroll through the exquisite market with my wife.

Chapter 7
What the next generation should be spared

Extreme existential experiences

Misfortunes in the family / Disappointments in the tax dispute / Success does not create friends alone

> *We are both among the last of a generation who have not yet made their last exit, who experienced World War II. We had experiences that caused us to encounter existential fears, obliteration and death at an early age. What memories do you have of it? What developed from it for your attitude to life?*

The insight that dominates today, that we cannot value highly enough the long period of peace and prosperity that we experienced in Germany and Europe since 1945. We even escaped the nuclear catastrophe that was feared in the so-called Cold War. We must communicate this insight to the next generation. It has – at least up to now – been spared what we had to get to know of the cruelties of war and its consequences.

These are extreme experiences with existential fear that you do not forget your whole life long. When I was nine years old, I was playing with friends in Austrasse street in Künzelsau. Suddenly a fighter-bomber came to attack the Kochertal railway. The pilot already began shooting with his aircraft cannon at the level of the buildings on the densely populated street. We children ran away from each other. I took shelter behind a low wall on the balcony on the ground floor of the house in Austrasse 13. If I had stood only three or four meters further to the left or to the right, I would have been shot dead. But a good angel protected me. In the street there were fifty-centimetre-wide holes from the bullets. The pilot shot and mortally wounded the locomotive driver on his train.

Now, when we see war images again on the television from Ukraine, bad memories come back. About a week after the large bomb attack by the Royal Air Force on Heilbronn in 1944, in which more than 6,000 people were killed, my father and I were travelling through the devastated city to Ilsfeld to my father's parents. Because rail and tram lines were interrupted, we had to go from Karlstor station to Südbahnhof station on foot.

There was a foul smell of burned flesh. I remember the zinc tubs that stood beside the mountains of debris on streets that had been cleared perfunctorily. There were burnt bodies lying in them, human bodies that had shrunk down to sixty centimetres. A horrific sight that has stuck with me and in me. That also has something to do with why I believe the unification of Europe to be so important as a peace project. And likewise the appeal for a new German policy towards Russia that I co-signed in November.

> *As an entrepreneur, you went from success to success, not shying away from risks, almost according to the Olympic motto: Faster, higher, further. But there were setbacks, there were disappointments, there were extreme situations – in the company and in your family. Do you talk about them?*

I cannot keep them a secret, I do not want to keep them a secret either. The decisive question is: Do you learn from them? I have always tried to learn from experiences. It sounds so trivial: We learn from life. But for me, it is a constant apprenticeship. I have remained inquisitive and eager to learn. Situations that you allude to with your question are also tests, of the capabilities of the entrepreneur, of personal physique and psyche, of the love that a family needs.

Risks are part of the entrepreneur like stamina is part of a marathon runner. I would not have become an entrepreneur if I was not prepared to and able to do it. I knew that there can be setbacks. At the beginning of the sixties, I had a formative experience in this. With our tempestuous growth of often 70 to 100 percent per year, liquidity was always scarce; the money was tied up in debtors and in the inventory. So I had overdrawn the credit account with the Volksbank yet again. The director summoned me one day and announced: "Würth, if you overdraw your account now one more time, then I will freeze the account, I will honour no more cheques and I will terminate the business relationship, I am certainly not going to let you destroy my pension." This experience affected me for my entire life: One of my most important principles was and is: Growth without profit is lethal.

As you know, I never took the Abitur, the school leaving examination. My father took me out of the secondary school in Künzelsau beforehand, when I was fourteen. I did not get to university until I assumed a professorship in entrepreneurship in Karlsruhe in 1999. I tried to pass on the entrepreneurial experience I had gathered in practice to the students there. This also includes the fact that you have to define and strive for goals for yourself and for your company for ten years into the future if possible. I never gave up my goals, even if they sometimes appeared unattainable and setbacks occurred now and again.

Shortly after the turn of the millennium, there was a general economic downturn that also affected the Würth Group in 2003. The first Iraq War came as well. We had to even let employees go. We reorganised the structure and the management of the Group. But I never gave up my optimism that we will achieve our goals: Where we are market leader, to expand our position, where we are not there yet, to become it.

Conclusion: Setbacks happen, but that cannot stop you from continuing to pursue your goals, from setting new goals. My goal has always remained to be better than the average.

> *That does not just make friends!*

Envy is one of the fruits of success.

> *Disappointments never fail to materialise either. How do you get over that?*

Disappointments are always painful. The confidence that they can be overcome and the knowledge that they are part of life help you to get over them. Disappointments also arise from your own mistakes, for example in personnel decisions. I had to pay dearly when I founded some of the foreign companies, like in the Netherlands, where I had put a man in charge of sales who did not accomplish anything because of his inexperience. Then I went to the customers in the Netherlands myself with another Dutch employee.

I was horrified when the first business year at Würth Austria had to be closed with a loss. At that time, I was in Vienna, extremely concerned; I browbeat the management into accepting a bill of exchange for half the loss. That was an effective disciplinary measure. In the following years, there were no more losses.

Disappointments arise too when you expect too much or excessively speedy success when developing new business fields. We established an electronics department in 1971, and it took years before the success was achieved that Würth Elektronik in Niedernhall has today. Many companies we acquired had to be restructured before they returned a profit. Today, Würth Elektronik is one of the best horses in our stable.

An important employee or a diligent employee hands in their notice, and you are disappointed and think that will trigger immense problems for the future. Five years later you realise: This resignation was the best thing that could have happened, simply because the position was discharged much better by a successor than was the case before. That is how disappointments can turn out to be successes with the passing of time.

The effects of the first oil crisis around 1975 shocked me. For the first time, I had to swallow a decline in sales, let employees go for the first time. We had liquidity problems, considerable debts outstanding at the foreign subsidiaries. In addition, I personally had to carry the costs of renovating Hermersberg Castle, which I had acquired as a family residence in 1970. The costs rose far above the planned levels. The banks limited our credit lines, and constantly checked we were adhering to them. Every day, a bank called and demanded we put money onto the overdrawn accounts. We discovered that we had neglected our planning during the times of exorbitant growth. We straightened that out, partly by leasing the real estate. In 1976, we started hiring again. From 1977, things were really looking up again. We learned from the crisis to restructure the company and to gear ourselves for growth at all levels in terms of organisation, planning and finances.

Just like you should not rest on your successes, neither should you let yourself be demoralised by setbacks. We gained a positive energy for our future from the setbacks and disappointments. Because successes cannot be the only thing that drives a company forward. Failures must also be analysed critically and questioned, and always with the goal of becoming even better, even more successful.

> *In 2007, a multi-million-euro tax fine was imposed on you. You have described publicly how deeply this tax affair shook you personally. You told the Bild newspaper in an interview that when you looked in*

the mirror in the morning, you saw a gangster there. What is the hard core you said you had to swallow?

Even today, I still feel extremely unfairly and unjustly treated. If I had known as much about criminal tax law then as I do now, the case would have taken a completely different course. If I had been younger and had had good legal representation, then the case would not have been allowed to close with a penalty order for peace sake. Instead, the case would have been taken through the levels of jurisdiction right up to the supreme court. The sentence still distresses me a lot today. The wound has now healed, but scars remain that hurt sometimes.

Did you yourself make no mistakes that partly triggered the case?

The case was predominantly about internal transfer prices and allocation of costs between the parent companies. Twelve tax audits had previously been carried out on precisely these procedures within a period of 30 to 40 years, without any objections.

I made mistakes in my choice of lawyers, was advised abysmally on the part of my lawyers. That was a catastrophe for me. When the tax inspectors' raid was taking place in my office, I was in a meeting at the Federal Chancellery in Berlin. When the tax investigators came to the office, there was not even a lawyer there. He had to be called from Stuttgart first. He evidently had not anticipated what was in store for us. And I ask myself, was it really a coincidence that I was not in the office at the time in question? Or had someone previously – by whatever means – taken a look into my diary? I myself was never questioned about the accusations. I later drove to the public prosecutor's office of my own volition.

My lawyer said to me: "… they are expecting you to get two years in the clink."

The lawyer lied to me in order to be able to sell what emerged as a compromise as his success afterwards. Today, after such a breach of confidence on the part of a lawyer, I would immediately revoke his appointment and find another lawyer! There were several other things too. Because I had a bad feeling myself, I wanted to call in an additional lawyer from Düsseldorf. Then the lawyer from Stuttgart blocked that too and explained to me that everything had already been negotiated with the public prosecutor. Consequently, the lawyer from Düsseldorf backed down of his own volition and said he did not want to intervene any more if it had progressed so far already. If the lawyer in Düsseldorf had got to see the files, if he had seen what was going on, then the outcome would have been completely different.

And another very important aspect was actually that I had been held liable although personally I was so far away from the company legally. In fact, I am no longer the owner at all. The taxes are paid by the family trusts. The company is owned by trusts. The authorities held me liable as if I was the owner of the company who is liable for everything. This aspect wrongly never came up in the discussion. That was how it turned out to be such a legal catastrophe.

Apart from that one meeting, I never spoke to the public prosecutor. I was also never questioned about any fact whatsoever. That was all done by the lawyer. I was also never questioned by the judge in Heilbronn who had issued the criminal order. He should really have called me to appear sometime. He should have questioned me about how I see the matter. But the lawyers said to him that they had negotiated all of that with Würth already. It was ready to be signed. It was a catastrophe.

> *It is certainly quite conspicuous that tax audits took place, financial statements were published and everything appeared to be all right for years. Then suddenly everything is reopened retrospectively. Was someone behind this? Who? Why?*

I do not know. I really do not know. But today I would no longer take a lawyer from the judicial district of the public prosecutor in charge of the case. Too many cryptic connections are involved there. You cannot avoid that at all if you work together for twenty, thirty years. I say, without wanting to put forward a theory, that wheeling and dealing took place that time. My chances would have been better, or at least fairer, with a non-resident lawyer.

Did the fact that politicians did not see themselves in a position to take corrective action also contribute to your disappointment? Did you expect that your philanthropic activities would be valued more highly?

Not necessarily among politicians, but among the media. I can understand that reticence prevails on the part of politicians in such cases. That too is part of constitutional behaviour, that politicians do not intervene in the justice system. Likewise, I expect from the media and from politicians that they protect the people concerned from being pilloried unjustly. That is also one of the jobs of a serious press.

At that time, I had a really lovely experience with German President Köhler. The Stuttgarter Zeitung newspaper had written that Würth should give back his Cross of the Order of Merit. Then the German President said: He is keeping his Cross of the Order of Merit. That was a little bit of balsam for my soul after all.

Back then, I experienced how true the saying is: "A friend in need is a friend indeed." In the negative press hype, most representatives of public life retrenched, with three exceptions. CDU Minister of Science Peter Frankenberg called me, CDU parliamentary party leader Stefan Mappus came to my office, and Greens politician Rezzo Schlauch visited me and encouraged me. I will always be grateful to these gentlemen for this.

You have often described yourself as a family man. Your employees experience this, thousands in the Würth Group experience this, when the entire family celebrates company parties with them, when you and your wife celebrate important birthdays in a large circle of employees. Thus the misfortunes which your family were not spared must have hit you all the harder. Can we talk about them?

My family and I have learned to cope with the fact that our son Markus has to live with a disability because of a medical mistake and our granddaughter Anne-Sophie lost her life at the age of eight in a traffic accident. That remains a constant pain. But I think I can say that I have to simply accept that without complaint. I am well aware of this: If someone is in the wrong place at the wrong time, then the same thing could have happened to anyone that happened to Anne-Sophie. My wife and I were happy when our daughters were born. And then, when our son Markus came along, I thought that I had been given the gift of a successor.

In the case of our son Markus one could really ask: How can a doctor make such a mistake? During a triple vaccination, when the first vaccination had caused a high temperature, to simply continue vaccinating although my wife expressly said, "I don't want to continue vaccinating because he had a temperature." And the doctor said: "Nonsense, that is such a healthy little chap, he looks so well, that won't do anything to him." He vaccinated for the second time, and then the disaster occurred. Markus had a high temperature for six months. His brain was severely damaged.

You can really only learn from this too. If I had any say in the matter, I would strictly forbid general practitioners from being allowed to vaccinate children. To my mind, that would be solely the task of paediatricians, because they have a better understanding of the little ones, after all, more specialist expertise. Later, when we spoke with doctors about our Markus case, they threw their hands in the air and said: "How could someone do that?"

Markus is such a sweet-natured person. It is a tragedy that a human life like this was almost destroyed by medical malpractice like this. But there is also no sense in asking: How can God allow such a thing? Because those are then the big questions in life towards which one must simply remain humble in one's own powerlessness. And one must also try to use this experience to help others who have to deal with a harsh fate. My wife, who has taken this particularly to heart, says that the ideas for this do not emerge in the head, but in the heart.

Markus lives in an anthroposophical village community. Our family supports this project financially through the Würth Foundation. Our daughter Bettina, who is currently the Chairwoman of the Advisory Board of the Würth Group, founded the Freie Schule Anne-Sophie schools in Künzelsau and in Berlin in memory of little Anne-Sophie. Bettina incorporated her educational experiences into the schools' guiding principles. They aim to empower children and young people with individual responsibility through education and training. The objective is to be able to live their lives successfully as distinctive personalities. Today (2015), as a comprehensive school, this school is taking 600 children right up to Abitur, the school leaving examination.

Here, too, we make our financial contribution through the Würth Foundation. My wife supports disabled people in Germany and abroad with her great strength and love. In 2003, my wife established the Hotel-Restaurant Anne-Sophie in Künzelsau, which collaborates with the sheltered workshops in Heilbronn and Ingelfingen. In doing so, she is pursuing her most important concern, to give the lives of disabled people meaning and fulfilment. Disabled people learn under educational and specialist supervision how to play a part in the working procedures of a gastronomy business.

The misfortunes that my wife and I experienced took us to the edge of our own existence. That makes you humble. We try to help others to overcome their misfortunes.

Chapter 8
Reinhold Würth the Christian

There is solace and hope in faith

Heaven is open to Hindus and the rich too / Creation is not a fluke of evolution / The social obligation of ownership in practice

> *Shortly before your 80th birthday, it is obvious you would think about the finite nature of life. Do you believe in a hereafter?*

Yes. But I do not know where it is and what I should or can imagine it to be like.

> *In our dialogues, you have repeatedly emphasised that you have become so tolerant because of your life and because of your travels, because of your encounters with other cultures, that you see the religions alongside each other and no longer in a hierarchy in the way that Christianity was communicated to us as the superlative of all religions. Has the hierarchy of religions with Christianity at the top, characterised by the history of salvation and enlightenment, been dissolved in your eyes?*

Certainly not. I definitely feel like a Christian. I was confirmed. Later I held the office of deacon for a while in our parish in Künzelsau. My father did some work for his parish. Going to service is part of Sunday in our family.

On our first holiday trip in our Opel Olympia, when we had a stopover in the Hanover area, I remember how my parents sent me to Lehrte to find out where the New Apostolic church was. I found it, and we all went to service together every Sunday.

I met my wife at a service in a New Apostolic church. She used to sing in her parish choir in Friedrichshafen. At that time, men and women still used to sit separately in the nave, the women on the left, the choir up at the front to the right of the alter. We were married on 9 December 1956 in the New Apostolic church in Künzelsau. Carmen wore her white veil deservedly. We had both been brought up as strict New Apostolics.

Even if I no longer go to church every Sunday – I belong to it. Even my grandparents were New Apostolics. We come from a region where there are traditionally many facets of Protestantism. You cannot simply throw out this heritage like a worn-out suit.

> *Faith gives the Christian strength to resist geriatric depression. Does that still apply in our time, which is characterised by this-worldliness?*

I believe so. There is something comforting in faith. And also something hopeful. That is expressed as a request in a beautiful prayer: Lord, give me a merciful death. My ideal image is that on a Sunday afternoon, in or around two-thirty, after a nice meal and a good glass of wine, I would fall asleep in the granddad armchair and not wake up any more. But we cannot choose how we go; we have to take what God decides.

Many people are afraid of geriatric depression because they have no tasks in their lives any more, for example that they will fall into a hole after they retire. I do not need to be afraid of this. People who are active can deal better with growing old. And they also generally live to be older than others who no longer know why they are alive.

The older I get, the more important my family becomes to me, with all its members, both living and no longer alive. I see myself as a link in a chain that reaches from my ancestors right up to my grandchildren, as part of a tribe whose roots are lost in the mists of time. I live off the roots of my parents, grandparents and great-grandparents. My ancestors were predictable, sound and reliable. Characteristics that I have made my own as a Christian.

Home *(Heimat),* family, faith in God are my sources of strength.

> *Do you have a Christian world view?*

I assume I have a Christian world view. I try to live according to the Christian rules. The Ten Commandments take top priority as practical instructions for this. I learned them when I was only a child, and later in confirmation class. They have always remained a guideline for me – even if life experience and the sober-mindedness that comes with it show us that there is probably no one who can manage to always live above reproach according to them. But that does not annul the Commandments; it does not make them less important. Precisely because we know human weaknesses, we also know how important the Commandments are. They are based on what we call conscience.

According to my observation, every person was given a conscience. It makes no difference here which religion a person belongs to, or whether they are in India or in Russia. Stealing is a negative everywhere and, however you define it, is classified as a sin. Everyone knows: Whoever takes something that does not belong to them has a bad conscience. I do believe that this conscience is integrated into man's genetics, as a fundamental gift for equipping man as a social being, so to speak. Strictly speaking, no religion is required for this. Every person carries a conscience within themselves and it gives them the capability to differentiate between what is right and what is wrong.

> *Doubt is also part of faith, and not just as a result of enlightenment. Are you free from this?*

Of course not. Our world gives us reason to doubt every day – and to despair of faith. In August 2014, I was at Hartmannsweilerkopf in Alsace when German President Joachim Gauck and French President François Hollande laid the foundation stone for a memorial. A hundred years ago in World War I, more than 30,000 soldiers died there on a little more than a square kilometre. They killed each other, they were cannon fodder. On both sides, among the French and us Germans, the pastors blessed the weapons and shouted to the soldiers: God be with us! But you do have to ask yourself then: Where was God at that time? That cannot have happened in his name.

> *The Bible contains the Apocalypse. The end of the world is a running theme throughout Christianity as a vision of horror and salvation.*

Today, humanity has developed ways to take away its means of existence from itself. It is becoming increasingly likely that thousands of nuclear bombs will not stay in their bunkers forever. At some stage, a mad person will trigger the nuclear catastrophe, and the adversary will retaliate with atomic bombs. Then maybe a few people will be left who have been bombed back into the Stone Age. Thousands of years will be needed again to reach the current level of technology. Maybe that is how you have to imagine it.

> *Maybe God has been very merciful to us after all by preventing that up to now.*

Hmm. The good God gave us reason, and if we use our reason correctly, then that is godly.

> *The Christian world view is based on the creation story in the Old Testament. Atheists say that no trace of a creator has been found in the cosmos up to now. Is evolution a fluke?*

The findings of the natural sciences surpass what we learned about Heaven and Earth as children from parents and grandparents, at school and in church. But I cannot simply imagine that this wonderful, wondrous system which we humans are, both physically and mentally, which for example we are only just getting to know through neurology and brain research, through genetics, that we humans are fluke results of our evolution. I believe that it is becoming clearer than ever from the findings of research that there is a Creator.

Thus the existence of a God is almost a matter of course for me. Whoever says, "There is no God" can prove that just as little as I can provide proof that there is a God. That is where we experience the difference between knowing and believing. The God question fills entire libraries. We cannot use our reason to find the solution. We can only approach faith.

When we attempt to envision the dimensions of the cosmos, then we realise how small we humans are, how little we know about ourselves and the world. The Milky Way, which continues to fascinate us with its billions of stars, is only a very small spiral nebula in the universe. How can we grasp the infinity of the universe with our concepts of time and space?

In my youth, the Big Bang was three billion years ago; today, people speak about eight billion years. What lies behind the universe? What was before the Big Bang? The findings we have discovered from science about the cosmos lead us simultaneously to the insight that we know very little about the emergence of our existence. That exhorts us to be modest. We must bow modestly with humility before the incomprehensibility of this creation, before the cosmos, before the time dimensions of the universe.

And that reminds us of a tenet of Christian faith: Where human wisdom stops, God's wisdom only starts. Through faith, we find a bridge into an understanding of our existence that cannot be grasped rationally, into the awareness of how limited our own time on this Earth is, how little we can imagine the eternity of creation or its end. We are exhorted to think about our death.

My theory is that only a God can have created such a wonderful universe, a being like the human, and of course the diversity of animals and plants too. I believe that evolution has an underlying creation idea. It is unimaginable to me that everything supposedly came about by itself, like a succession of coincidences in evolution. Yet I have no problem accepting Darwin's theory of evolution – a million, a hundred million years make no difference to God, so that the question of the chronology of events is totally irrelevant.

That includes the question: Are there intelligent beings on other stars? I can scarcely imagine that in these billions and billions of stars we people on our own little Earth are the only beings who can reflect on themselves. Maybe there are millions of other cultures who are 500,000, 50 million, 500 million years further on in their development. It is quite possible that some beings have found a possibility to actually travel faster than light. My friend Harald Unkelbach, who is a doctor of mathematics, said recently in one of our conversations that there are initial theses that it could actually be possible to travel faster than light.

> *Do you not view creation as a development which has not yet been completed?*

The creation story is a magnificent tale that helps us to get a picture of the evolution of the world. There are stories like this about our origin in almost all cultures and religions. We can interpret them.

To me, creation is a process, a development, to which the expansion of our knowledge through the natural sciences also belongs. It is imminently possible that other intelligent beings who reflect on themselves live in the cosmos. We still know much too little. And we cannot be sure that we will not destroy our means of existence on Earth ourselves, for example, if some mad person starts the final nuclear war. Stephen Hawking did not prophesy for no reason that humanity only has one chance to survive: that is, if it could settle on another planet. He might be right.

Does the insight into the limits of our knowledge lead to religion?

I believe so. The God question fills many libraries, and has preoccupied scholars from all religions. Our reason always takes us to limits – to new, expanded limits. Then the zone begins in which our rational explanations end.

Many religions claim the truth for themselves alone. The Christian churches were and are not free from this in their dogmas. How can this be reconciled with the tolerance that you count among your life rules?

I am almost 80 years old now. A lot of experience has accumulated with other cultures and religions. I am on the board of trustees of Hans Küng's World Ethos Foundation. I may define myself as a Christian, but I am against every claim to sole representation when it comes to religion. I respect every religion. I agree with Prussian King Frederick II, that everyone should become blessed in their own way. Thus I expect from people of different faiths the respect for my Christianity with which I for my part encounter their attitude.

What we are experiencing now on the part of the terrorists of the so-called Islamic State in the Middle East and in parts of Africa, that is horrible insanity. Fortunately, leading Muslims in Germany have made it plain that this terrorism is exploiting Islam to establish a dictatorship of terror. My point is that no-one has sole access to Heaven. I mean, a Muslim or a Jew or a Buddhist or a Shintoist can get into Heaven, into their Heaven, just as easily as we Christians can get into ours.

Christianity took a long time to permit itself this insight. Even general human rights were not recognised by the powers that be in Christianity for a long time, not to mention protected. Doesn't our image of the Christian person still have a few rather dark stains?

Too many people who wanted to transcend the Middle Ages in Christianity and enforce the Enlightenment were excommunicated or ended up with their heads on the block. The derivation of the individual's right to freedom from the Christian image of the person and from the principle that the freedom of the individual person is inviolable, because it comes from God – that has only been generally recognised as an insight in the last hundred years. That human rights are based on God-given basic rights, and are not at the disposal of any state, any government, any human power – that is a lovely principle from which large, if not the largest parts of the world are still far removed.

When I think back to my youth, the difference between the Protestants and the Catholics was still hugely pronounced, well, those were still really confrontational circumstances. Or when you think of the gays, the lesbians – I mean, that would have been unthinkable fifty years ago, that a gay man would become the mayor of Berlin. It would have been crazy, there would have been uproar, and today all that is totally normal.

> *Our generation grew up in a time when Christianity determined the secular order in society with light and dark. The Christian environment, the bonds to the churches, the familiarity with Christian commandments are dissolving in Europe. What will remain? Which role remains for the churches?*

The fact is that the proximity to churches, the bonds to the churches are declining quite rapidly, and in fact to the extent that people's lives are improving. People have become more independent and self-assured. They decide themselves and individually where they used to allow themselves be led by churches and other institutions.

In our experience, God is in demand in times of hardship. Then people seek the connection to the churches again too. In this day and age, where there is effectively no hardship, where no one in Germany has to starve or freeze, God is not necessarily in demand. That is deliberately a general statement to illustrate a trend. I do not overlook the fact that we have to help where there are people who need our help here in Germany too. That will become a growing task. Not because I assume that direct hardship is in store for us Germans. I am thinking here about the burgeoning migration that is confronting the wealthy countries in Europe with the hardship in Africa and the Middle East. The rapidly rising number of people who seek asylum here in Germany puts us in a dilemma between the Christian commandments of helping the poor and oppressed on the one hand and the limits of our propensity for economic generosity and cultural tolerance on the other hand.

> *Christianity is not losing its attraction everywhere in the world to the same extent that it is in Europe. When the Pope says a mass in the Philippines, millions of Catholics gather, likewise in Latin America. In Africa, the Protestant communities are increasing.*

That confirms my conclusion that people who suffer hardship – physical or psychological – turn to the place where faith promises them solace and strength in a way they can understand. To that extent you can say that the rejection of the churches in Europe is a wealth phenomenon.

> *Are small church communities retaining a stronger cohesion than the big churches, are they developing more bonding forces for their community members? How are you experiencing that in the New Apostolic community?*

I notice that attendance is declining in the New Apostolic Church too; but in relative terms, meaning in percent, definitely less than in the big churches. Nevertheless, some church buildings have been closed in the New Apostolic Church, here in the area too, and parishes have been merged, on grounds of rationalisation, because there simply weren't as many parish members any more. Church faith is being put to the test here too.

I was in Malta recently. We inaugurated a new plant and celebrated 25 years of Würth Malta. One of my best friends lives there, a Catholic priest. He is a fighter, an incredibly amiable, sporty person who approaches people, who simply wins people over and inspires them. He built a new church – made it really modern and trendy. Everything was paid for. He has between 70 and 90 percent of the seats occupied at every mass. It is no longer like that in Malta either any more. The example shows: Wherever the church presents what it has to offer in a people-friendly way, the faithful will come into the churches. That is a Catholic example, and it is no different in the New Apostolic Church. Wherever people feel they are being addressed correctly, they will happily accept what the church has to offer.

> *It says in the Bible that it is easier for a camel to go through the eye of a needle than for a rich man to enter the kingdom of God. Not a good prospect for you…*

Yes – I was taught that already back in confirmation class, that we should not set ourselves the goal of material wealth, but intellectual, or even better: spiritual wealth. I cannot imagine that rich people are excluded from the kingdom of Heaven on principle. Surely that would not be Christian either.

> *What does money mean to a rich person like you, who can afford everything that is for sale?*

For me personally: Money is actually irrelevant. I have more watches than I can wear on my arm; I have two iPhones and iPads. Money – that is printed, note-sized paper.

> *What protects you from the temptation to use wealth primarily as power?*

Humility, modesty, the insight about the finite nature of our human life, the recognition of the Ten Commandments. If you do not have high principles, power is a dangerous drug. Whether they want to or not, it will always put people in danger of becoming arrogant. And then they won't notice it themselves. I sincerely hope that I managed not to let myself be corrupted by the power of success.

> *You drive your companies to constant growth. But that actually means: more capital, more wealth?*

Without growth in competition, in global completion, we endanger the jobs that we created together with our employees. Our wealth – that is now the Würth Group's €3.6 billion in equity capital. This capital is in the companies of the Würth Group, everywhere, in the investments, in the plants, in the buildings. The aim is not personal enrichment. The aim is to give the Würth Group the foundations for its future. An earthly goal – but in it lies the responsibility of the entrepreneur. Maybe even a particular responsibility of the Christian entrepreneur which always includes the jobs that several thousand families are relying on.

My wife and I, my entire family, see ourselves as having a social obligation. That corresponds to our Christian attitude. That is also the recognition of the social obligation of ownership that is in the Basic Law (the German constitution).

The social obligation of ownership is also stated in the set of rules and regulations that prescribes binding standards for the entire Würth Group beyond my time. With our trusts, my wife and I have taken on tasks of caring for the weak in society, of promoting young talents, of establishing schools here in the region and in other states, of caring for people with disabilities.

That may not be as well-known as the Würth Group's art collections that we make accessible to the public free of charge in the art forums, as the activities in the area of universities or the prizes for literature and music. But we practice here what we are very happy to fulfil as an obligation in society. We thus enable others to participate in our wealth. In doing so, we attempt to find the compromise between securing the future of the companies in the Group and our employees' jobs on the one hand and accepting responsibilities in society on the other hand.

On the one hand, the company should and must increase its equity capital to secure its future and to be able to create new jobs. That too is a contribution to the benefit of society as a whole – that we have created around 66,000 jobs. On the other hand, the current situation of the world cannot be forgotten. After all, we do want to contribute just a little bit to a better world – even if we know that we could not save the world if we were to relinquish all our wealth. It seems to be the way of the world that the rich are getting increasingly richer. That is why, although I am and will remain a liberal, I do not deny the state the right to regulatory intervention.

> *A little bit of Christian social teaching is expressed in the social obligation of ownership as stipulated in the Basic Law (the German constitution). Is that still relevant today in a multicultural society?*

That was certainly a central motivation when the Federal Republic of Germany was being established and the Basic Law was being decided. Today, this aspect should not be over-cultivated. We have a great many Muslim entrepreneurs in Germany, also a large number of Jewish ones, and quite certainly still more for whom there are absolutely no ties to any religious conviction. But the Basic Law is an obligation for everyone, including the Hindus and the atheists.

Today, the attitude to this commandment in our constitution is more a question of personal conscience than of religion. In an open society, the social obligation of ownership corresponds to human logic and humanist teaching; it becomes tangible in the jobs that arise out of ownership. This can be summarised as follows: Eighty or maybe even ninety percent of the social obligation of ownership is securing jobs and creating new jobs.

> *In your speeches and lectures, you advocate modesty as a virtue time and again. A Christian virtue? What is political modesty, in your opinion?*

For the Christian, it is a virtue to act with humility and modesty. In politics, modesty means: Deliberately renouncing the power that one could exercise. Modesty generates respect and sets an example. And it is also frequently adopted for imitation.

I believe that the exemplary nature of modesty is incredibly important for relationships – not just within politics, but also in the family, in the firm, in the company, among friends, among acquaintances. People who exercise modesty are viewed amiably, are perceived to be pleasant and people feel good around them.

> *Max Weber established a very useful connection between religion and capitalism in his book about the Protestant ethic. He described impressively how the wealth of the merchants in Holland came about after the Reformation, meaning through the reconciliation of economic success with a life that is pleasing to God. Thus wealth is the reward that one can already receive on earth as a Christian for handling earthly goods responsibly. It appears to me that you have made Max Weber's ethic the principle for your actions.*

I devoted myself a lot to Max Weber, particularly during the time at the University of Karlsruhe when I taught entrepreneurship. I learned a lot from Max Weber, for myself in my personal orientation, but also for my understanding of our economic system, its strengths and its hazards.

Weber elaborates the difference between Catholicism and Puritan Protestantism in great detail. That resonates up to today in Württemberg in Puritanism and Pietism. Weber took away from material success the repugnance of the discrepancy to living according to Christian faith principles. But that was not all: He derived from that the obligation to handle material success responsibly.

Weber sees in work the foundation of every form of safeguarding human existence. He does not demonise wealth which results from ambitiousness, entrepreneurial courage and commercial skill. But at the same time he exhorts moderation and abstinence from waste. One can say that Max Weber's ethic is highly modern, particularly in light of the excesses of banks and financial conglomerates.

However, Max Weber's findings on the foundations of economic success, which are still valid, also teach us: If one was to give away everything that the rich own, the poverty in the world would not be abolished. The world would become poorer. The value added that constitutes the economic means of existence for a growing number of people only emerges through work and the increase of capital.

Naturally, I also ask myself the question: Where on earth is capitalism heading? Where is the end? Trees cannot grow into the sky. There are limits to growth in our economies too. That is logical. But – where are they? Sometimes it seems like there is no limit to wealth in this world.

However, world history shows that neither a global empire nor a dynasty has become increasingly richer into the future unchecked. Obstacles come up somewhere; wrong decisions are taken – internally or externally. Let us remember Charlemagne or Napoleon in political history, or the Fuggers, the Rothschilds or the Krupps in economic history. It was always a matter of becoming, being and decaying. That is why I always have the triptych "Life – Nature – Death" by the painter Giovanni Segantini from Graubünden in my mind's eye. It expresses a fateful development of our existence that no one and nothing can evade. Not only the individual people are subject to it, but also world empires, companies, banks, dynasties, parties and churches.

Chapter 9
Dialogue with Bettina Würth

Women manage differently

But the aims of the Advisory Board Chairwoman are the same as the father's: All the power for the company

> *When your father reaches his 80th birthday, increased public attention will be directed to the future management of the Würth Group. The change in generations will take place in a time when women are still the exception as company managers. Like you!*

I have been Chairwoman of the Advisory Board of the Würth Group for nine years. In that respect, no change in generations is on the cards in our company. My father ensured continuity in the company management at an early stage when he transferred the chair of the Advisory Board to me and he himself took over the chair of the Supervisory Board of the Würth Group's family trusts, which are the owners of the company.

> *Politicians are introducing a women's quota for leading positions in business. What do you think of that?*

Nothing!

> *Why?*

Because, yet again, this is tantamount to discrimination. Quotas are something different to having the same conditions for men and women in decisions about management positions. I was never able to determine if the male colleagues would have had any objections to entrusting a management position to a woman.

> *Do women manage differently to men?*

Yes, women are more cooperative. We think and work in a more networked manner than men. That also differentiates the management style. We see the team more than the individual frontman. Men often have too much tunnel vision. They see a problem and an objective, look for the solution and march off. Then they often do not notice what has been left behind or passes by on the right or on the left. Emotions also play a role that has to be considered. If that does not happen, a rework will be necessary which could have been avoided in the run-up.

> *Maybe political force really is needed to achieve a breakthrough to more women in management positions?*

A quota is the wrong way. It does not lead to the goal which I too advocate. Anyone who wants to give women more opportunities in their job has to create the prerequisites for that in society. Attempts have been made here for many years. Women must be given the opportunity to combine job and family. There is still a lot lacking. If women know where they can put their children and know their children are being well looked after, they can operate freely and develop differently in their professional lives than if these conditions do not exist. I also do not think that the politicians' assumptions are correct that are based on an image of women that propagates professional advancement primarily as women's path in life. The image of women should not be developed in only one direction. We have to accommodate the various life models. More part-time jobs are needed for this, more childcare facilities. That is more important than female quotas.

> *Hohenlohe, the Group's home (Heimat), recruits employees who are asked to come here from other regions. When families move, the women also want job opportunities. What is your experience with this?*

We are in an area here where there is pretty much zero unemployment. When we want to recruit skilled personnel, we often do not find the perfect fit immediately, because the people who are 25 or 30 years old have no ties yet, as in no family. They want to live in cities and urban regions. Then the range of childcare facilities available for children does not help either.

> *Your call for choices for women does not just place demands on politicians. Without corresponding provisions in business, it will remain wishful thinking. What do you do about it at Würth?*

We already have many part-time jobs. Working hours are becoming increasingly more flexible. We are currently setting up childcare facilities. In 2015 we will establish a day-care centre in the Freie Schule Anne-Sophie school. Some of the companies already have one. We want solutions for the entire Group. We are a family-run company. And we are an employee-friendly company and in this respect we are also indirectly a family-friendly company of course. Because when we deal with the needs of our employees respectfully and attempt to be an employer who cares about its employees' wellbeing, questions like "How does one reconcile private life and business matters?" are automatically incorporated.

> *Your father established the Würth Group. Your father shaped it. You are treading in big footsteps. Do you notice how critical looks are directed at you from outside?*

I do not let myself become unsettled by what you observed as critical perceptions from outside. The expectations that come to a head in the question, "What is going to happen after Reinhold Würth?" have attended us for years. I am sensitive on that point. I know that that could also entail temptations to sow discord. Then one could sit back and wait: Just look at how those two are getting on together. I will not let myself be pushed down this road. My father and I have the development quite well under control. We have already been living the change in company management for some years now. And it is going well. I rise to every challenge. When I say yes to a position, then it means yes!

At the beginning of 2006, my father officially announced that he wanted to pull back a little from the company and work less, and that his daughter would succeed him. I had already been with the company for a long time. Mr Friedmann, the Chairman of the Central Managing Board, was brand new in his position back then. At that time, we probably pushed ahead somewhat with great zest such that my father sometimes felt ignored on some issues or even side-lined.

But: With all due respect to what he has created – I am not treading in my father's footsteps. That is not possible either. That would be as if you wanted to masquerade as someone else by putting on a different suit.

I am putting all my energy into the company and I am pursuing the same goals as my father. I want to maintain our culture, which he shaped. I want – like him – to secure the achievement orientation and the performance potential in the entire company for the future. That is definitely the biggest task that emerges from a transition like this.

But I do not have to do it in the same way my father did. I have my own style and my own management techniques. I am a very pragmatic worker. I want the Würth Group to continue growing, yield profits, achieve sales growth and maintain and create secure jobs.

My father and I work well together. Each of us performs their tasks competently. Years of discovery, that were not always easy, lie behind this, both in my father's case and mine. That is the aspect of interpersonal relations.

I have never made a secret of the fact that we have also had disputes. If that was not the case – then something would definitely have been wrong. When my father celebrated his work anniversary in 2014, that is, celebrated working for the company for 65 years, we performed an ironic sketch of my father's application for a job in the Group. As a native of Hohenlohe, he has a great sense of irony. And he laughed with us, when we made fun of him and his personality.

On the other hand, my father packed the company brilliantly into a secure structure. He placed it into four family trusts and created a splendid set of rules and regulations for them. The owner functions are amalgamated and the family structure is reflected in the Supervisory Board. The nine-person Advisory Board, of whom I am the Chairwoman, supervises and supports the Group's business operations. The guidelines of business policy are drawn up by the Central Managing Board. Every executive body knows what it has to do, what responsibility it has been assigned, what decision-making powers it has been granted. We have quite a bit of experience under our belts in this constellation already – and it works. That was difficult sometimes too, but I found my way.

> *What do you see as the entrepreneurial family tradition?*

To me, a family tradition is the way we behave, for example. Thus, for me and my children, there is a tradition of behaving the way we were brought up to do by my parents. And I hope that the culture will be practiced in my family too that we practice in the company, like for example honesty, directness and modesty. I am pleased when my children show an interest in the company. Whether they will get involved in the company, and how – they have to decide that for themselves.

> *Many company founders find it hard to deal with non-family management. You are the next generation after your father and directly connected to the Central Managing Board as Chairwoman of the Advisory Board. How do you manage this task in practice?*

We have a management that is not part of the family. That works well. I see us as a team where every member has their function. I work on the same level as my colleagues on the Central Managing Board.

> *When you talk about the company's culture, you include achievement orientation. What do you mean by that?*

Our corporate culture includes all of the internal and external actions. I ensure that we all take on this challenge again and again. We want to be successful, work professionally, aggressively and at the same time modestly. All of that is reflected in flat hierarchies.

We have high performance requirements in the company for everyone who works here. That means: to give more than the usual. On the other hand, we also want to give back more for the performance. That applies to the financial side, but also to the diverse development opportunities in the company and to the way we interact with one another. Those are principles of our employee management. The employees are perceived as people. That also includes that they are given help in emergencies. A lot of energy is required to achieve all that.

> *Where do you draw your energy from?*

From the will to fulfil the tasks that I have taken on and am facing up to. My father's succession, which I have assumed, must be visible. The employees must feel that they are being managed. Energy should not be wasted, it must be used adeptly. Using manpower sensibly, that creates acknowledgement. That occurs when my colleagues and my employees notice that I am working with them on the current issues, that I am fighting for the company with them, that they get feedback from the Chairwoman of the Advisory Board.

Do you have role models? From whom do you get advice?

A very close role model: my mother. She says outright what she thinks is right and what she thinks is wrong. She is the heart of our family. I also get advice from my father and I discuss things with my colleagues. My husband is a good advisor too. But ultimately I have to decide alone. And I stand behind the decision that I have made.

The Group is working on the conversion to e-commerce. How are you approaching this challenge?

That is more difficult for us than, for example, the mail order business, which operates more with catalogues in the market and less with direct sales than we do. Our salespeople are with customers every day. That has been our practice for over sixty years. The company is geared to having consignees in the form of its sales force. They serve the customers with the information they receive every day and expedite the orders to the benefit of the company. That has always been very successful. Our entire sales expertise is out in the market every day. Now electronics are changing customer behaviour and the market. That requires adjustments in our company.

What does that mean precisely?

The customers were way ahead of us. They used the internet more intensively than we could offer it to them. That is why the topic swept over us so quickly. We are putting a lot of resources and a lot of energy into this conversion and are occupied with answering questions like the following ones: How is our customers' purchasing behaviour changing? What do we ask of our salespeople? How many salespeople will we need out in the market in future? The business model is changing, but not as dramatically as was feared a year ago.

We have clearly defined our commitment: Even in the age of the internet, the sales force is our indispensable selling power. We want to further strengthen the core competencies that we have acquired. That is an important signal for the employees.

There is still a lot of potential in the market that can and must be leveraged with our business model. We want to increase our market share. We have more than 100,000 products in our range. There is still enough for the salesperson to offer the customer. But that only works if we benefit the customer with it. This is where the advice from the salesperson comes into play as a strength. In this area, tradespeople will remain our key clientele.

> What role does product development play in your company? Are you constantly working on product innovation?

It plays a large role, often in collaboration with suppliers. We frequently get suggestions from innovators, inventors and tradespeople which we adopt and implement. Our developments are primarily improvements to tools and to fastening systems. That can, for example, be a better drive point on screws that means that patio wood does not split any more when screws are driven in, and thus no one can get hurt by splinters any more when they walk over it.

> Your father also represents the image of the Group through his high public profile. You are conspicuously reticent in this regard.

I see my primary task as developing what constitutes the culture here in the Group –achievement, reward of achievement, respect towards and for one another, customer orientation, innovative capabilities. In this way I contribute to helping develop the company. This requires a high internal profile and commitment to the company. Appearing in public – other people can do that too. And that also already occurs often and on many levels for the company.

Of course I know that I will not always be able to elude the public role. I will face that when I decide that it is necessary. But I do not have to do it in the same way and at the same intensity as my father. That matches his personality, he does it well, he enjoys it and therefore is authentic. One can only be good at what one feels authentic doing. My father's long-time friend, Rolf Bauer, has never given a public speech. But that did not detract from his importance to the company. Incidentally, I also perform a large range of functions outside the company already in my own way.

For example?

I am Vice-President of the German-Swiss Chamber of Commerce. I was Vice-President of the Heilbronn-Franken Chamber of Industry and Commerce, am currently on the Executive Committee of the Federation of German Industries, or BDI, and on the Steering Committee of the Economic Council of the CDU. I initiated the Freie Schule Anne-Sophie school in Künzelsau. I contribute to the Business and Industry Advisory Board of the Goethe-Institut, Germany's cultural institute that operates worldwide.

> *Your father integrated art into the working world. With the forums and museums in the company's industrial premises. He puts into practice – most visibly in the Kunsthalle Würth art gallery in Schwäbisch Hall – the motto of the former Frankfurt city councillor in charge of cultural affairs, Hilmar Hoffmann: Culture for everyone. Admission is free, children get special fostering in art appreciation. Do you include that in your understanding of tradition?*

That is part of us, part of our brand image. The task remains to maintain the art collection and publicise it more. I will exert influence to ensure that that continues to be practiced actively and cultivated in the Group's self-image. But I will not take it on personally. That is and will remain the company's task.

Publications by Reinhold Würth

The archive of the Würth Group made the following extensive bibliography available for this book.

Books

Reinhold Würth (1985), *Beiträge zur Unternehmensführung [Thoughts on Company Management]*. Schwäbisch Hall: Swiridoff Verlag, ISBN 3-921279-07-0.

Reinhold Würth (1985), *Thoughts on Company Management*. Schwäbisch Hall: Swiridoff Verlag, ISBN 3-921279-08-9.

Architekten-Wettbewerb, Verwaltungsgebäude der Adolf Würth GmbH & Co. KG [Architecture Competition, Headquarters of Adolf Würth GmbH & Co. KG] (1987). Schwäbisch Hall: Swiridoff Verlag.

Reinhold Würth (1995), *Erfolgsgeheimnis Führungskultur – Bilanz eines Unternehmers [Management Culture: The Secret of Success – An Entrepreneur Takes Stock],* Frankfurt/New York: Campus-Verlag, ISBN 3-593-35266-4, Künzelsau: Swiridoff Verlag, 2nd Edition 1999, ISBN 3-934350-08-9.

Reinhold Würth (1995), *Management Culture: The Secret of Success – An Entrepreneur Takes Stock.* Frankfurt/New York: Campus Verlag, ISBN 3-593-35421-7.

Reinhold Würth, *Entrepreneurship in Deutschland – Wege in die Verantwortung [Entrepreneurship in Germany – the Paths to Responsibility],* Writings of the Inter-Faculty Institute for Entrepreneurship at the University of Karlsruhe (TH), Vol. 1. Künzelsau: Swiridoff Verlag, ISBN 3-934350-32-1.

Reinhold Würth (Ed.) (2001), *Wer wagt? – Unternehmensgründungen in Deutschland [Who Dares? – Business Start-Ups in Germany],* Writings of the Inter-Faculty Institute for Entrepreneurship at the University of Karlsruhe (TH), Vol. 2. Künzelsau: Swiridoff Verlag, ISBN 3-934350-44-5.

Reinhold Würth (Ed.) (2001), *Strömung der Zeit – Wirtschaft und Gesellschaft an der Schwelle zum 21. Jahrhundert [The Tides of Change – Business and Society on the Threshold of the 21st century],* Writings of the Inter-Faculty Institute for Entrepreneurship at the University of Karlsruhe (TH), Vol. 3. Künzelsau: Swiridoff Verlag, ISBN 3-934350-45-3.

Reinhold Würth & Hans Joachim Klein (2001), *Wirtschaftswissen Jugendlicher in Baden-Württemberg– Eine empirische Untersuchung [Knowledge of Economics Among Adolescents in Baden-Württemberg – An Empirical Study],* Writings of the Inter-Faculty Institute for Entrepreneurship at the University of Karlsruhe (TH), Vol. 4. Künzelsau: Swiridoff Verlag, ISBN 3-934350-46-1.

Reinhold Würth (Ed.) (2003), *Wirtschaftsunterricht an Schulen im Aufwind? [Economics Lessons in Schools on an Upswing?]* Writings of the Inter-Faculty Institute for Entrepreneurship at the University of Karlsruhe (TH), Vol. 7. Künzelsau: Swiridoff Verlag, ISBN 3-89929-013-5.

Reinhold Würth (Ed.) (2003), *Wer wagt, gewinnt! Unternehmensgründungen in Deutschland [Who Dares, Wins! Start-Ups in Germany],* Writings of the Inter-Faculty Institute for Entrepreneurship at the University of Karlsruhe (TH), Vol. 8. Künzelsau: Swiridoff Verlag, ISBN 3-89929-001-1.

Reinhold Würth (Ed.) (2004), *Wirtschaftswissen in der Lehrkräftefortbildung [Economics in Teachers' Further Training],* Writings of the Inter-Faculty Institute for Entrepreneurship at the University of Karlsruhe (TH), Vol. 11. Künzelsau: Swiridoff Verlag, ISBN 3-89929-050-X.

Reinhold Würth, Wolfgang Gaul & Viktor Jung (Ed.) (2005), *The Entrepreneurship-Innovation-Marketing Interface, Proceedings of the Symposium in Karlsruhe.* Künzelsau: Swiridoff Verlag, ISBN 3-934350-60-7.

Editorial contributions in books, magazines and collected editions

Was macht ein Unternehmen als Arbeitgeber attraktiv? [What makes a company attractive as an employer?] (1990). In Alexander Demuth (Ed.), *Imageprofile 1991 "Unternehmenskultur"* (S. 63–74) *[Image Profile 1991 "Corporate Culture" (pages 63–74)].* Düsseldorf: Econ Verlag, ISBN 3-430-14942-8.

Reinhold Würth & Günter Kraut (1991), Unternehmensführung – Quo vadis? [Company Management – Quo vadis?] In *Tübinger Universitätsreden Band 42, Die Verleihung der Ehrensenatorenwürde, Ansprachen anläßlich der Feiern am 22.02. und 25.03.1991* (S. 17–27) *[In Tübingen University Speeches, Vol. 42, the Award of the Honorary Senatorship, Speeches to mark the celebrations on 22 February and 25 March 1991 (pages 17–27)].* Tübingen: Attempto Verlag.

Strategie und Vision am Beispiel der Würth-Gruppe [Strategy and Vision Taking the Example of the Würth Group] (1991). In Prof. Dr. Erich Zahn (Ed.), *Auf der Suche nach Erfolgspotentialen – Strategische Optionen in turbulenter Zeit, Tagungsband zum Stuttgarter Strategieforum 1991* (S. 121–129) [Searching for Success Potential – Strategic Options in Turbulent Times, conference transcript of the Stuttgart Strategy Forum 1991 (pages 121–129)]. Stuttgart: Schäffer-Poeschel Verlag, ISBN 3-7910-0579-0.

Unternehmenskultur und Motivation [Corporate Culture and Motivation] (1992). In Richard Matheis (Ed.), *Erfolgsmanagement 2000, Konzepte für Menschen, Märkte, Unternehmen* (S. 296–307) [Success Management 2000, Concepts for People, Markets, Companies (pages 296–307)]. Frankfurt: F.A.Z.; Wiesbaden: Gabler, ISBN 3-409-19154-2.

Die Logistik im Spannungsfeld zwischen Führungstechnik und Unternehmenskultur [The Conflicting Imperatives of Management Technique and Corporate Culture in Logistics] (1992). In Bundesvereinigung Logistik e.V. (Ed.), *Tagungskatalog zum Deutschen Logistikkongreß '92 in Berlin, Logistik – Lösungen für die Praxis, Berichtsband über den Kongreß '92, Band 1* (S. 323–334) [Conference Catalogue for the German Logistics Congress '92 in Berlin, Logistics – Solutions for Practical Application, Proceedings from the Congress '92, Vol. 1 (pages 323–334)]. Munich: Huss-Verlag GmbH.

Festvortrag: Führungskultur als neue Dimension des Erfolges [Ceremonial Address: Management Culture – a New Dimension of Success] (1992). In Hans-Jörg Bullinger, Fraunhofer-Institut für Arbeitswirtschaft und Organisation (IAO) (Ed.), *Informationsarchitekturen als strategische Herausforderung: Lean Management, Integrationsmanagement, Informationsmanagement* (S. 9–21) [The Strategic Challenge of Information Architectures: Lean Management, Integration Management, Information Management (pages 9–21)]. Baden-Baden: FBO – Fachverlag für Büro- und Organisationstechnik GmbH, ISBN 3-922213-22-7.

Buchbesprechung [Book review], Marketing-Management 7th Edition 1992, by Philip Kotler/Friedhelm Bliemel (1992). In *M & M Marktforschung & Management, Zeitschrift für marktorientierte Unternehmenspolitik, (1)*, S. 37 f. [M & M Market Research & Management, Magazine for Market-Oriented Corporate Policy (1) (page 37 f.)].

Thesen zur Unternehmensführung im Jahr 2010 [Propositions for Company Management in 2010] (1993). In Günter Würtele (Ed.), *Lernende Elite: Was gute Manager noch besser macht* (S. 86–110) [The Learning Elite: What Makes Good Managers Even Better (pages 86–110)]. Frankfurt: F.A.Z.; Wiesbaden: Gabler, ISBN 3-409-19177-1.

Unternehmens-, Führungs- und Kommunikationskultur [Corporate, Management and Communication Culture] (1993). In Frank-Jürgen Witt (Ed.), *Managerkommunikation* (S. 17–26) [Manager Communication (pages 17–26)]. Stuttgart: Schäffer-Poeschel Verlag, ISBN 3-7910-0673-8.

Vorwort [Preface] (1993). In Siegmar Saul, *Führen durch Kommunikation* (S. 7 f.) [Leadership Through Communication (page 7 f.)]. Weinheim and Basel: Beltz Verlag, ISBN 3-407-36307-9.

Karrieremarketing im mittelständischen Unternehmen [Career Marketing in a Medium-Sized Company] (1993). In Organisationsforum Wirtschaftskongreß Köln (Ed.), *Die Ressource Mensch im Mittelpunkt innovativer Unternehmensführung* (S. 59–69) [People as Resources at the Focus of Innovative Company Management (pages 59–69)]. Wiesbaden: Gabler, ISBN 3-409-19195-X.

Die Osteuropa- und China-Strategie der Würth-Gruppe [The Würth Group's Eastern European and China Strategy] (1993). In Bruno Tietz & Joachim Zentes, *Ost-Marketing/Erfahrungspotentiale osteuropäischer Konsumgütermärkte* (S. 193–206) [Eastern Marketing/Potential for Experience in Eastern European Consumer Goods Markets (pages 193–206)]. Düsseldorf: Econ-Verlag, ISBN 3-430-19068-1.

Dienstleistung als Herausforderung für Führung und Unternehmenskultur [Service as a Challenge for Management and Corporate Culture] (1993). In Hermann Simon (Ed.), *Industrielle Dienstleistungen* (S. 309–317) [Industrial Services (pages 309–317)] Stuttgart: Schäffer-Poeschel Verlag, ISBN 3-7910-0655-X.

Unternehmensentwicklung und Mitarbeitermotivation in sich wandelnder Zeit [Company Development and Employee Motivation in Changing Times] (1993). In *Jahresbericht '93 Verband Fenster und Fassade* (S. 17–24) [Annual Report 93, Association of Window and Facade Companies (pages 17–24)].

Innovationswert der Marke im Befestigungsteilemarkt [The Innovation Value of the Brand in the Fastening Parts Market] (1994). In *Markenartikel – Zeitschrift für Markenführung, (5),* S. 227f. [Magazine for Brand Leadership (page 227 f.)].

Der Visionär mit dem Dickkopf [The Stubborn Visionary] (1994). In Horst Rückle, *Mit Visionen an die Spitze – zukunftsorientiert denken, handeln und führen* (S. 197–201) [Visions for Leadership – Future-Oriented Thought, Actions and Management (pages 197–201)]. Wiesbaden: Gabler, ISBN 3-409-19089-9.

Marketing nach innen [Inward Marketing] (1995). In Friedhelm W. Bliemel (Ed.), *"Mehr Markt" in der Unternehmensführung, Praxisbeispiele und Konzepte* (S. 28–42) ["More Market" in Company Management, Practical Examples and Concepts (pages 28–42)]. Berlin: Erich Schmidt Verlag, ISBN 3-503-03817-5.

Einführung [Introduction] (1995). In Hans Peter Schwarz, *Würth – Die Architektur weiterbringen (S. 9–43) [Würth – Promoting Architecture (pages 9–43)].* Munich: Aries Verlag, ISBN 3-920041-63-1.

Der Verkäufer als Botschafter des Unternehmens [The Salesperson as the Company's Ambassador] (1995). In *Zukunft Verkauf – neue Wege für Ihren Erfolg, 15 Experten verraten ihre Erfolgskonzepte* (S. 60) [The Future of Sales – New Methods for Your Success, 15 Experts Reveal their Recipes for Success (page 60)]. Würzburg: Max Schimmel Verlag, ISBN 3-920834-38-0.

Unternehmensphilosophie [Corporate Philosophy] (1995). In Jean-Christophe Ammann (Ed.), *Kulturfinanzierung, Dokumentation des Symposiums zur ART*

Frankfurt 1995 (S. 45–58) [Cultural Financing, Documentation from the Symposium at the ART Frankfurt 1995 (pages 45–58)], Regensburg: Lindinger + Schmid, ISBN 3-929970-17-1.

Unternehmenskultur leben und weitergeben [Living and Passing On Corporate Culture] (1995). In H.-J. Warnecke & H.-J. Bullinger (Ed.), *Fabrikstrukturen im Zeitalter des Wandels – welcher Weg führt zum Erfolg?* (S. 43–58) [Factory Structures in an Era of Change – Which Road Leads to Success? (pages 43–58)]. Berlin, Heidelberg, New York: Springer, ISBN 3-540-60722-6.

Der Faktor Mensch im Service [The Human Factor in Service] (1995). In *AT & T EdgeWare, Zeitschrift für Dienstleistungen im Bereich Computing & Telekommunikation, (1),* S. 18 f. [AT & T EdgeWare, Magazine for Services in the Area of Computing and Telecommunications (1) (page 18 f.)]

Geleitwort [Foreword] (1995). In Klemens Kappe (Ed.), *Effizienz durch Menschlichkeit; Neue Personalpolitik zur Gesundung der Unternehmen* (S. 9–13) [Efficiency Through Humanity; New Personnel Policy to Help Companies Return to Health (pages 9–13)], Stuttgart: Kreuz Verlag, ISBN 3-7831-1400-4.

Schaffung strategischer Wettbewerbsvorteile in sich wandelnder Welt [Creating Strategic Competitive Advantages in Changing Times] (1996). In *Schmidt Colleg News, (1),* S. 16–20 [pages 16–20].

Firmenkonjunktur statt Marktrezession! [Corporate Momentum Instead of Market Recession!] (1996). In *ASU/BJU Unternehmerzeitschrift, (4),* S. 18 [*ASU/BJU Entrepreneurs' Magazine (4) (page 18)*].

Geleitwort [Foreword] (1996). In Uwe Kirst & Stefan Bieler, *Unternehmensnachfolge, Über vier Hürden zur gesicherten Nachfolge* (S. V f.) [Company Succession, On Four Hurdles to Assured Succession (page V f.)]. Neuwied: Hermann Luchterhand Verlag, ISBN 3-472-02607-3.

Lehrpläne der kaufmännischen Schulen in kürzeren Intervallen modernisieren [Modernising Curriculums in Commercial Schools at Short Intervals] (1997). In *Festschrift des Verbandes der Lehrer an Wirtschaftsschulen in Baden-Württemberg* (S. 41–44) [Commemorative publication of the Association of Teachers in Business Schools in Baden-Württemberg (page 41-44)]. Ettlingen.

Irrationalität und Unternehmensführung [Irrationality and Company Management] (1997). In Adolf Würth GmbH & Co. KG (Ed.), *Kultur bei Würth, Beiträge zur Kulturarbeit in einem Unternehmen* (S. 7–33) [Würth and the Arts, A company's commitment to culture (page 7-33)]. (2., erweiterte Auflage [2nd extended edition] 1999). Künzelsau: Adolf Würth GmbH & Co. KG.

Irrationality and Company Management (1997). Adolf Würth GmbH & Co. KG (Ed.), *Wurth and the Arts, A company's commitment to culture* (S. 7–33). Künzelsau: Adolf Würth GmbH & Co. KG.

Würth – Motivation und Vision im virtuellen Unternehmen [Würth – Motivation and Vision in the Virtual Company] (1997). In Dr. Wieselhuber & Partner (Ed.), *Handbuch Lernende Organisation – Unternehmens- und Mitarbeiterpotentiale erfolgreich erschließen* (S. 507–514) [Manual for a Learning Organisation – Tapping Corporate and Employee Potential Successfully (pages 507–514)]. Wiesbaden: Gabler, ISBN 3-409-18694-8.

Kunst und Unternehmen – Das Beispiel Würth und Podiumsdiskussion mit Jean-Christophe Ammann, Gernd Schwandner, Michael Lingner und Reinhold Würth [Art and the Company – The Example of Würth and Panel Discussion With Jean-Christophe Ammann, Gernd Schwandner, Michael Lingner and Reinhold Würth] (1996). In Patrick Werkner et. al. (Ed.), *Kunst – Raum – Perspektiven, Ansichten zur Kunst in öffentlichen Räumen. Dokumentationsband des gleichnamigen Symposiums vom 21.–23.11.1996 in Jena* (S. 130–136 und S. 139–149) [Art – Space – Perspectives, Views of Art in Public Spaces, Documentation from the symposium of the same name from 21-23 November 1996 in Jena (pages 130–136 and 139–149)]. Jena: Kulturamt, ISBN 3-930128-29-2.

Die Zukunft des Mittelstandes im neuen Europa [The Future of Medium-Sized Business in the New Europe] (1997). In Frankfurter Allgemeine Zeitung GmbH, Junkers Bosch Thermotechnik (Ed.), *Standpunkte für ein grenzenloses Europa, Symposium am 15. September 1997 in Dresden* (S. 76–101) [Viewpoints for a Borderless Europe, symposium on 15 September 1997 in Dresden (pages 76–101)]. Frankfurt am Main.

Schaffung strategischer Wettbewerbsvorteile in einer sich wandelnden Welt [Creating Strategic Competitive Advantages in Changing Times] (1997). In Manfred Perlitz, Andreas Offinger, Michael Reinhardt & Klaus Schug (Ed.), *Strategien im Umbruch, Neue Konzepte der Unternehmensführung* (S. 19–25) [Strategies in Transition, New Concepts for Company Management (pages 19–25)]. Stuttgart: Schäffer-Poeschel Verlag, ISBN 3-7910-1192-8.

Gesellschaftspolitik in Deutschland am Ende des 20. Jahrhunderts [Social Policy in Germany at the End of the 20th Century] (1998). In Roland Ermrich (Ed.), *100 Jahre Ludwig Erhard. Das Buch zur Sozialen Marktwirtschaft* (überarbeitete Auflage) (S. 102–106) [100 Years of Ludwig Erhard. The Book on Social Market Economy (revised edition) (pages 102–106)]. Düsseldorf: MVV Medien Vertriebs- und Verlagsgesellschaft mbH, ISBN 3-9805581-0-X.

Als Mittelständler zur Weltmarktführerschaft [World Market Leadership for a Medium-Sized Company] (1998). In *Peter W. Weber (Hrsg.), Leistungsorientiertes Management* (S. 45–54) [Peter W. Weber (Ed.), Performance-Oriented Management (pages 45–54). Frankfurt am Main, New York: Verlag, ISBN 3-593-36078-0.

Verinnerlichte Ziele und lebendige Visionen sind die Voraussetzung für eine überdurchschnittliche Personalentwicklung [Internalised goals and vibrant visions are the prerequisite for outstanding personnel development] (1998). In Gerd Krakowitzer (Ed.), *Organisationskultur – Der Weg zum neuen Mitarbeiter, Qualitätsforum 1998* (S. 145–158) [Organisational Culture How to Attract New Employees, Quality Forum 1998 (pages 145–158)]. Leoben (Austria): Quality Management Institute, ISBN 3-929383-26-8.

Zukunftssicherung durch Familienstiftung – Praxisfall 6: Würth-Gruppe [Securing the Future With a Family Trust – Case Study 6: Würth Group (1998). In Gerhard und Lore Kienbaum Stiftung, Holger Sobanski & Joachim Gutmann (Ed.), *Erfolgreiche Unternehmensnachfolge – Konzepte – Erfahrungen – Perspektiven* (S. 259–265) [Successful Company Succession – Concepts – Experiences – Perspectives (pages 259–265)]. Wiesbaden: Gabler, ISBN 3-409-13102-7.

Vom Familienbetrieb zum Weltmarktführer [From Family Business to World Market Leader] (1999). In Erich Zahn & Stefan Foschiani (Ed.), *Maßgeschneiderte Strategien – der Weg zur Alleinstellung im Wettbewerb* (S. 79–92) [Customised Strategies – How to Achieve a Unique Position Among the Competition (pages 79–92)]. Stuttgart: Schäffer-Poeschel Verlag, ISBN 3-7910-1463-3.

Kunst, Kultur und Unternehmen – Das Beispiel Würth [Art, Culture and Company – The Example of Würth] (1999). In Klaus Götz, Monika Löwe, Sebastian Schuh & Martina Szautner (Ed.), *Cultural Change, Managementkonzepte Bd. 4* (S. 103–118) [Cultural Change, Management Concepts, Vol. 4 (pages 103–118)]. Munich and Mering: Rainer Hampp Verlag, ISBN 3-87988-386-6.

Entrepreneurship in Theorie und Praxis [Entrepreneurship in Theory and Practice] (2000). Die Entwicklung der Würth-Gruppe [The Development of the Würth Group]. In *Karlsruher Transfer, (24)*, S. 30–33 [Karlsruher Transfer, Business Journal of the Karlsruhe Institute of Technology (KIT) (24) (pages 30–33)].

Faktoren für die erfolgreiche Unternehmensführung im 21. Jahrhundert [Factors for Successful Company Management in the 21st Century] (2001). In Gustav Bergmann & Gerd Meurer (Ed.), *Best Patterns – Erfolgsmuster für zukunftsfähiges Management* (S. 17–20) [Best Patterns – Success Patterns for Future-Proof Management (pages 17–20)]. Neuwied: Hermann Luchterhand Verlag, ISBN 3-472-04600-7.

Die Öffentlichkeitswirkung von Kunstaktivitäten – Das Beispiel Würth [The Publicity Effect of Cultural Activities – The Example of Würth] (2001). In Hilmar Hoffmann (Ed.), *Kultur und Wirtschaft, Knappe Kassen – Neue Allianzen* (S. 135–143) [Culture and Business, Empty Coffers – New Alliances (pages 135–143)] Cologne: DuMont, ISBN 3-7701-5876-8.

Architecture at Würth, Architektur bei Würth (2001). Gottfried Knapp, & Andreas Schmid, *Building for the World – Architecture at Würth; Bauen für die*

Welt – Architektur bei Würth (S. 6–11 [pages 6–11]). Künzelsau: Swiridoff Verlag, ISBN 3-934350-43-7.

Neue Gründer braucht das Land [The Country Needs New Founders] (2001). In *Karlsruher Transfer, (25),* S. 5 f. [Karlsruher Transfer, Business Journal of the Karlsruhe Institute of Technology (KIT) (25) (page 5 f.)].

Zum Weltmarktführer hochgeschraubt – Ein Gespräch mit Prof. Dr. Reinhold Würth [Drilling the Way Up to World Market Leader – A Conversation with Prof. Dr. Reinhold Würth] (2001). In Peter May, Gert Sieger & Gerold Rieder (Ed), *Familienunternehmen heute – Jahrbuch 2002* (S. 75–79) [Family-Owned Companies Today – 2002 Annual (pages 75–79)]. Bonn: INTES Akademie für Familienunternehmen, ISBN 3-9808036-0-0.

Erfolgsgeheimnis Führungskultur [Management Culture – A Success Secret] (2001). In Josef Wieland (Ed.), *Human Capital und Werte – Die Renaissance des menschlichen Faktors* (S. 63–73) [Human Capital and Values – the Renaissance of the Human Factor (pages 63–73)]. Marburg: Metropolis Verlag, ISBN 3-89518-354-7.

Wirkliches Vorbild [A Real Role Model] (2002). In *entrepreneurmagazin, (1/2),* S. 44 f. [Entrepreneur Magazine, (1/2) page 44 f.].

Über den Zusammenhang zwischen Kunst, Kultur und Unternehmenserfolg [On the Connection Between Art, Culture and Corporate Success] (2002). In Torsten Blanke, *Unternehmen nutzen Kunst* (S. 142–148) [Companies Using Art (pages 142–148)]. Stuttgart: Klett-Cotta, ISBN 3-608-94054-5.

Vom Nutzen des Kultursponsoring für die Unternehmensgruppe Würth [On the Benefits of Cultural Sponsoring for the Würth Group of Companies] (2002). In G. Braun (Ed.), *Stadt Karlsruhe – Kultur; Kultur und Wirtschaft – Kultursponsoring international* (S. 143–149) [City of Karlsruhe – Culture; Culture and Business – International Cultural Sponsoring (pages 143–149)]. Karlsruhe: DRW-Verlag, ISBN 3-7650-8291-0.

Außendienstfluktuation und ihre Folgen [Sales Staff Turnover and Its Consequences] (2002). In *Karlsruher Transfer* (28), S. 10 f. [Karlsruher Transfer, Business Journal of the Karlsruhe Institute of Technology (KIT) (28) (page 10 f.)].

Lähmende Bürokratie – Ursächliche und hemmende Einflüsse [Paralysing Bureaucracy – Causal and Obstructive Influences] (2002). In Martin Bacher, Fritz Spielberger (Ed.), *Dreigliederung oder Bolschewismus* (S. 75–83) [Threefold Order or Bolshevism (pages 75–83)]. Schorndorf: Verlag Carl Bacher, ISBN 3-924431-39-6.

Unternehmensethik und Unternehmenskultur als Schlüssel zum Erfolg [Corporate Ethics and Corporate Culture as the Key to Success] (2004). In Alexander Brink & Olaf Karitzki (Ed.), *Unternehmensethik in turbulenten Zeiten – Wirtschaftsführer über Ethik im Management* (S. 223–238) [Corporate Ethics in Turbulent Times – Business Leaders On Ethics in Management (pages 223–238)]. Bern, Stuttgart, Wien: Haupt Verlag, ISBN 3-258-06791-0.

Globalisierung der Geschäftsidee – Das Fallbeispiel Würth [The Globalisation of a Business Idea – Case Study Würth] (2004). In Joachim Zentes & Bernhard Swoboda (Ed.), *Fallstudien zum Internationalen Marketing, Grundlagen – Praxiserfahrungen – Perspektiven* (S. 105–118) [Case Studies in International Marketing, Principles – Practical Experience – Perspectives (pages 105–118)]. Wiesbaden: Gabler, ISBN 3-409-21513-1.

"Made in Germany" (2004). In *Diplomatisches Magazin, (4)*, S. 32 f. [Diplomatic Magazine (4) (page 32 f.)]

Implementing SAP R/3 Financial Accounting (2004). In Henning Kagermann (Ed.), *Realtime – A Tribute to Hasso Plattner, Beitrag in der Festschrift zum 60. Geburtstag* (S. 9–14) [Realtime – A Tribute to Hasso Plattner, Article in the commemorative publication to mark his 60th birthday (pages 9–14)]. Indianapolis, Indiana: Wiley Publishing, Inc., ISBN 0-7645-7108-7.

Chancen und Aufgaben von Familienstiftungen [Opportunities and Tasks for Family Trusts] (2004). In Christian G. Böllhoff, Michael W. Böllhoff, Wilhelm A. Böllhoff & Marili Ebert (Ed.), *Management von industriellen Familienunternehmen, Beitrag in der Festschrift zum 70. Geburtstag von Dr. Wolfgang Böllhoff* (S. 273–275) [Managing industrial family-owned companies, article in the commemorative publication to mark the 70th birthday of Dr. Wolfgang Böllhoff (pages 273–275)]. Stuttgart: Schäffer-Poeschel Verlag, 3-7910-2403-5.

Vorwort [Preface] (2004). In Hans Joachim Braun (Ed.), *Schrauben, Fügen, Kleben – Zur Entwicklung der Befestigungstechnik*; Schriftenreihe der Georg-Agricola-Gesellschaft Band 29. Freiberg [Screwing, Assembling, Gluing – On the Development of Fastening Technologies; series of papers of the Georg Agricola Society, Vol. 29, Freiburg]. ISBN 3-931730-10-7.

Führungskultur und Erfolg – Bilanz eines Unternehmers [Management and Success – An Entrepreneur Takes Stock] (2004). In Jörg Schlüchtermann, Hermann-Josef-Tebroke (Ed.), *Mittelstand im Fokus – 25 Jahre BF/M-Bayreuth* (S. 323–335) [Focus on Medium-Sized Companies – 25 Years of BF/M-Bayreuth (pages 323–335)]. Wiesbaden: Deutscher Universitäts-Verlag/GWV Fachverlage GmbH, ISBN 3-8244-8019-0.

Unternehmenskultur – Führungskultur – Menschenführung [Corporate Culture – Management Culture – Leadership] (2004). In: *Vorträge zum Festakt 100 Jahre Gerling* (S. 22–25) [Lectures Marking the Celebration of 100 Years of Gerling (pages 22–25)]. Cologne.

Mut, Kreativität, Verantwortung – Gedanken eines baden-württembergischen Unternehmers zur Unternehmenskultur [Courage, Creativity, Responsibility – Thoughts of a Baden-Württemberg Entrepreneur on Corporate Culture]

(2005). In Agrarsoziale Gesellschaft e.V. (Ed.), *Landwirtschaft in Verdichtungsräumen* (S. 21–26). Schriftenreihe für Ländliche Sozialfragen, Band 145 [Agriculture in Conurbations (pages 21–26). Series of papers for rural social questions, Vol. 145]. Göttingen. ISSN 0080-7133.

Vorwort [Preface] (2005). In Günther Somnia, *Abenteuer Umsatz. Helmut Gschnell und die Erfolgsgeschichte von Würth Italien* [*The Sales Adventure. Helmut Gschnell and the Würth Italy Success Story*]. Neumarkt: Würth Italien, ISBN 88-901691-0-9.

Ohne Eigentum ist alles nichts [Everything is Nothing Without Ownership] (2006). In Schwäbisch-Hall-Stiftung (Ed.), *Kultur des Eigentums* (S. 129–134) [The Culture of Ownership (pages 129–134)]. Bibliothek des Eigentums, Band 3 [Vol. 3]. Berlin: Springer Verlag, ISBN 978-3540-33951-9.

Die Öffentlichkeitswirkung von Kunstaktivitäten – Das Beispiel Würth [The Publicity Effect of Cultural Activities – The Example of Würth] (2007). In Wolfgang Schneider (Ed.), *Grundlagentexte zur Kulturpolitik* (S. 237–242) [Basic Texts on Cultural Policy [pages 237–242)]. Hildesheim: Glück & Schiller Verlag, ISBN 978-3-938404-119.

Grußwort / Greeting (2007). In: Union Mittelständischer Unternehmen e.V. – UMU (Ed.), *Europäischer Elite-Mittelstandspreis – The European Elite SME Award 2007* (S. 12–14 [pages 12–14]). Munich.

"Human Capital" – der wichtigste Produktionsfaktor [Human Capital – the Most Important Production Factor] (2007). In Gerd Swiss, Ulrich Iberer, Helmut Keller (Ed.), *Lernen am Unterschied* (S. 37 – 52) [Learning From the Difference (pages 37–52)]. Bielefeld: W. Bertelsmann, ISBN 978-3-7639-3574-1.

Was Familienunternehmen auszeichnet und gefährdet – Erfolgsfaktoren für unternehmerisches Handeln [What Distinguishes and Endangers Family-Owned Companies – Success Factors for Entrepreneurial Actions] (2007). In: Verband Baden-Württembergischer Omnibusunternehmer (WBO) e.V. (Ed.), *Festreden anlässlich der WBO-Jahrestagung am 16. November 2007* (S. 16–22) [Speeches to Mark the Annual Conference of the WBO on 16 November 2007 (pages 16–22)]. Böblingen.

Vorwort [Preface] (2007). In Justus Frantz, *Virtuos führen (S. V–VII)* [*Virtuosic Management (page V–VII)*]. Munich: Hanser Verlag, ISBN 978-3-446-40968-2.

Erfolgreiche Unternehmensführung in sich verändernder Zeit [Successful Company Management in Changing Times] (2009). In Ingrid Göpfert (Ed.), *Logistik der Zukunft – Logistics for the future* (S. 251–262) (5. Auflage) [pages 251–262; 5th Edition]. Wiesbaden: Gabler, ISBN 978-3-8349-1085-1.

Kunst und Geld – Antipoden oder Feinde? [Art and Money – Antipodes or Enemies?] (2009). In Annette Kehnel (Ed.), *Geist und Geld* (S. 11–21) [Muse and Money (pages 11–21)], Frankfurt am Main: Frankfurter Allgemeine Buch, ISBN 978-3-89981-211-4.

Vorwort [Preface] (2011). In: Steffen Merz (Ed.), *Die Faszination des Fliegens. Der Würth-Flugbetrieb 1966–2011* (S. 4 f.) [The Fascination of Flying. The Würth Aviation Business 1966–2011 (page 4 f.)]. Künzelsau: Swiridoff Verlag, ISBN 978-3-89929-232-9.

Der Dübelpapst – ein "Phänomen" [The Rawlplug King – a "Phenomenon"] (2012). In *Werner Fuchs, Jan Hofmann (Ed.), Befestigungstechnik, Bewehrungstechnik und …; Rolf Eligehausen zum 70. Geburtstag* (S. 25–28) [Fastening Technology, Reinforcement Technology and …, To Mark the 70th Birthday of Rolf Eligehausen (pages 25–28)]. Stuttgart: ibidem Verlag, ISBN 978-3-8382-0397-3.

Vorwort [Preface] (2012). In: *Am Drücker! Mitarbeiter porträtieren ihr Unternehmen anlässlich 50 Jahre Würth Österreich* (S. 9) [Fingers on the Button! Employees Give a Portrayal of Their Company to Mark 50 Years of Würth Austria (page 9)]. Künzelsau: Swiridoff Verlag, ISBN 978-3-89929-241-1.

Vorwort [Preface] (2012). In: Thilo Baum, Martin Laschkolnik (Ed.), *Die Bildungslücke. Der komprimierte Survival-Guide für Berufseinsteiger* (S. 3) [The Education Gap. The Condensed Survival Guide for Young Professionals]. Kulmbach: Börsenmedien Verlag, ISBN 978-3-942888-96-7.

Von der Pike auf lernen, bescheiden und dankbar zu sein [Learning to Be Modest and Grateful From the Start] (2014). In Frank Arnold, *Der beste Rat, den ich je bekam* (S. 221–223) [The Best Advice I Ever Received (pages 221–223)], Munich: Hanser Verlag, ISBN 978-3-446-43872-9.

Books about Reinhold Würth

Karlheinz Schönherr (3. Aufl. 2001), *Nach oben geschraubt. Reinhold Würth. Die Karriere eines Unternehmers [Drilling Your Way To the Top. Reinhold Würth. The Career of an Entrepreneur]*. Künzelsau: Swiridoff Verlag, ISBN 3-934350-33-X.

Ute Grau und Barbara Guttmann (2005), *Reinhold Würth. Ein Unternehmer und sein Unternehmen [Reinhold Würth. The Entrepreneur and His Company]*. Künzelsau: Swiridoff Verlag, ISBN 3-89929-057-7.

Silvia Zulauf (2014), Spüren, was stimmt. Zum 65. Arbeitsjubiläum von Reinhold Würth [*Sense What's Right. On Reinhold Würth's 65th Company Jubilee*] Künzelsau: Swiridoff Verlag, ISBN 978-3-89929-299-2.

Curriculum Vitae Prof. Dr. h.c. Reinhold Würth

Chairman of the Supervisory Board of the Würth Group's Family Trusts

The curriculum vitae compiled here represents an extract from the more extensive collection of data which was provided to the publishers from the archive of the Würth Group.

20 April 1935 born in Öhringen.

1949   At 14, first apprentice in his father's screw wholesalers in Künzelsau, commercial apprenticeship as a wholesaler, examination in 1952.

1954   Death of father Adolf Würth; Reinhold Würth takes over the small business with two employees. The first business year under his management (1955) closes with a double-digit increase in sales, with annual sales of 170,000 DM. Using the favourable circumstances of the reconstruction boom after World War II, the company starts operating throughout the Federal Republic of Germany.

1956   Marriage to Carmen Linhardt.

1962   Establishment of the first foreign subsidiary in the Netherlands. Today, the Würth Group has operations in over 80 countries with more than 400 companies and employs more than 66,000 staff; sales in 2014 were € 10.1 billion.

1985   Cross of the Order of Merit of the Federal Republic of Germany.

1987   Business Medal of the State of Baden-Württemberg.

02/1991   Honorary senator of the Eberhard Karls University in Tübingen.

1991	Opening of the new company headquarters building in Künzelsau/Gaisbach with Museum Würth, where the Würth art collection is made accessible to the public free of charge. Architects: Siegfried Müller and Maja Djordjevic-Müller.
1993	Reinhold Würth retires as managing associate from operational management and takes the chair of the Advisory Board of the Würth Group.
1994	Medal of Merit of the State of Baden-Württemberg.
1996	Officer's Cross of the Order of Merit of the Federal Republic of Germany.
1997	Honorary citizenship of the city of Erstein/France.
1999	Honorary doctorate (Dr. rer. pol. h.c.) from the Eberhard Karls University in Tübingen.
06/1999	Appointment as honorary professor of the University of Karlsruhe (TH).
1999	At the University of Karlsruhe, Reinhold Würth establishes the Interfaculty Institute for Entrepreneurship. He heads the institute until the end of the summer semester in 2003.
2000	French "Chevalier dans l'Ordre des Arts et des Lettres" medal in recognition of particular services for the proliferation and dissemination of French art and culture.
2001	Opening of Kunsthalle Würth in Schwäbisch Hall. Architect: Henning Larsen.
2003	Acquisition of the Fürstenberg Collection with works by Medieval masters.
2003	Honorary citizenship of the city of Künzelsau to Reinhold and Carmen Würth.

2004	Knight of the Order of the Legion of Honour (Chevalier de l'Ordre de la Légion d'Honneur).
2004	Ludwig Erhard Medal (awarded by the Ludwig Erhard Foundation, Bonn, for services to the social market economy).
2004	German Founders' Award 2004 in the category "Life Achievement" awarded by StartUp, an initiative of German savings bank association Deutscher Sparkassen- und Giroverband, McKinsey & Company, stern, ZDF.
2006	Chair of the Advisory Board of the Würth Group passes from Reinhold Würth to Bettina Würth.
2007	Honorary doctorate from the University of Palermo in Art History.
2007	Honorary doctorate from the University of Louisville, Kentucky, United States.
2008	Opening of the renovated Johanniterkirche church in Schwäbisch Hall as home to the Old Masters from the Würth Collection.
2008	Opening of the Musée Würth in Erstein (France).
2009	First recipient of the Röntgen Medal from the Julius Maximilian University in Würzburg, awarded to mark the opening of the Adolf Würth Centre for the History of Psychology.
2009	Award of the "Mercury," the highest honour of the Heilbronn-Franken Chamber of Industry and Commerce.
2009	Award of the "Grand Golden Medal of Honour" of the district of Hohenlohe.
2009	Awarded the University Prize by the Eberhard Karls University Tübingen as part of the Dies Universitatis.

2009	Officer of the Order of Arts and Letters (Officier de l'Ordre des Arts et des Lettres) in recognition of outstanding services to cultural collaboration between Germany and France.
2012	Officer of the Legion of Honour.
2012	Award of the 3rd James Simon Prize to Reinhold and Carmen Würth in Berlin.
2012	The Holbein Madonna acquired for the Würth collection becomes part of the exhibition in the Johanniterkirche church in Schwäbisch Hall.
2013	Commander of the Order of the Legion of Honour (Commandeur de l'Ordre de la Légion d'Honneur).
2013	Internationaler Folkwang Prize, Essen (awarded by the Folkwang Museumsverein).
2013	Prix Europe 2013 from the Académie Rhénane, Strasbourg.
2013	Honorary Senator of the University of Heilbronn.
2013	Opening of the Würth Forum in Rorschach (Switzerland).
2014	Sales of the Würth Group exceed the € 10 billion mark for the first time.
2015	Honorary citizen of the city of Schwäbisch Hall.

The author

1936 born in Würzburg; studied in Basle, Munich, Hong Kong. Honorary senator of the European University Viadrina Frankfurt (Oder). Member of the jury for the German-American Radio and Television Awards of the Rias Berlin Commission. Book publications include: "Die anderen Deutschen – Wie der Osten die Republik verändert" (The other Germans – how the East is changing the Republic). Professional background (excerpt): senior editor at Deutsche Welle; general manager of the Ludwigshafen pilot project to introduce private radio and television; secretary general of Federation of German Newspaper Publishers (BDZV); joint editor of Donaukurier newspaper, Ingolstadt; editor of the Märkische Oderzeitung newspaper; publisher of the Haller Tagblatt newspaper.